Gluten-Free
on a
Shoestring

Gluten-Free
on a
Shoestring

125 Easy Recipes for Eating Well
on the Cheap

Nicole Hunn

Da Capo
LIFE
LONG

New York

Copyright © 2011 by Nicole Hunn
Photography by Lisa Weatherbee

Editorial production by *Marra*thon Production Services. www.marrathon.net
Design by Jane Raese
Set in 11-point Archer

Cataloging-in-Publication data for this book is available from the Library of Congress.

First Da Capo Press edition 2011
ISBN 978-0-7382-1423-8

Published by Da Capo Press
A Member of the Perseus Books Group
www.dacapopress.com

Note: The information in this book is true and complete to the best of our knowledge. This book is intended only as an informative guide for those wishing to know more about health issues. In no way is this book intended to replace, countermand, or conflict with the advice given to you by your own physician. The ultimate decision concerning care should be made between you and your doctor. We strongly recommend you follow his or her advice. Information in this book is general and is offered with no guarantees on the part of the authors or Da Capo Press. The authors and publisher disclaim all liability in connection with the use of this book. The names and identifying details of people associated with events described in this book have been changed. Any similarity to actual persons is coincidental.

Da Capo Press books are available at special discounts for bulk purchases in the U.S. by corporations, institutions, and other organizations. For more information, please contact the Special Markets Department at the Perseus Books Group, 2300 Chestnut Street, Suite 200, Philadelphia, PA, 19103, or call (800) 810-4145, ext. 5000, or e-mail special.markets@perseusbooks.com.

To the best-laid plans.
To the ones I love.

Contents

3. Kitchen Confidence: Basic Recipes That Serve as the Foundation for Many Others

8. Room for Dessert: Cakes, Cookies, and Pies   *181*

Contents

Life is sweet and fun.
Gluten is expendable.

Introduction

It's no surprise that, no matter how spacious the house, guests and family members always head for the kitchen like homing pigeons. That's where all the action is. And it's the cook who sets it in motion.

A good meal can leave a lasting impression; it can even make your day. And turning out a favorite dessert can make an otherwise ordinary meal into something memorable. All you need is some standard kitchen equipment, plus a few basic skills and recipes, and you're on your way. When you have the ability to cook, you can reward yourself and your family with homemade treats, tailoring every last detail to your own tastes. You can perk up your entire office with a simple batch of cookies or cupcakes. Or cater to a child's special birthday wish. Bake a loaf of bread, and you'll make any house smell like a home. As long as your pantry is well stocked with the basics, nothing is out of reach. And none of that has to change when you're gluten-free.

First, a few basics. Gluten is the protein found primarily in wheat, barley, and rye. It is found in *all* conventional breads and pastas and is also frequently hidden in ingredients such as maltodextrin and dextrin, hydrolyzed vegetable protein, malt or malt flavoring, and modified food starch, all of which are often derived from gluten-containing ingredients. Increasingly, there are all sorts of people who eat a gluten-free diet in varying degrees, from the strictly gluten-free to the occasional gluten-free foods dabbler. Celiac disease is an autoimmune disease in which, in response to the ingestion of gluten, the body attacks itself by destroying villi, the fingerlike projections in the lining of the small intestine that are responsible for absorption of nutrients. The only treatment is to follow a completely gluten-free diet. Recent research indicates that celiac disease affects as many as 1 in 133 Americans, most of whom remain undiagnosed. Many others who do not have celiac disease choose to enjoy the benefits of a gluten-free diet as well, including those suffering from nonceliac gluten sensitivity, family members of celiacs, and those seeking various other general health benefits from the diet. Whether you're new to eating gluten-free and fear that the creative foodie part of your life is gone forever, or you've been gluten-free for a while and have resigned yourself to lowered expectations and expensive, store-bought gluten-free foods that leave you cold, help is on the way. Everything's going to be just fine.

All that being said, I must admit that it took me loads of trial and error to come to this state of Gluten-Free Zen. When we discovered that my second child, Jonathan, had celiac disease, although I was thankful his condition didn't warrant a lifetime of expensive medications with possible side-effects, I honestly didn't know the first thing about eating gluten-free. And I worried about how his dietary restriction would affect our entire family. So I started out by sticking with naturally gluten-free foods like vegetables, meats and vegetarian proteins, like rice and beans. The only baking I was confident enough to try was with gluten-free mixes. At the time, I thought mixes were my only hope, and, frankly, I was grateful to have them. Without much experience with conventional mixes upon which to base my expectations, I just gave it a whirl. I don't want to tell tales out of school and spell out exactly which brands I tried, but suffice to say that there was some weeping (me) and some queasiness (me, the kids, my husband). And there was also the whole unpleasantness (my husband and me) about how much these experiments were costing us (a lot). I paid over $6.00 for a gluten-free cake mix, plus the cost of shipping, and the cost of the ingredients that I had to add to the mix to make the cake. King Arthur Flour's gluten-free bread mix costs $8.99—just for the mix! But I took it on the chin and kept searching, assuming I just hadn't yet stumbled upon the right mix.

And, time and time again, our thoughts turned wistfully to sandwiches. Initially we relied on packaged gluten-free bread. I remember this one particular bread that could be cured of that dense, gluten-free sponginess by toasting it. The only problem was that you had to eat it within moments. If you took the time, all 5 minutes of it, to actually make a simple turkey sandwich, the bread would spring back to its pretoasted, spongy form. I have to imagine that if a company set out intending to make bread with such unyielding resilience, they would have failed miserably.

I tried looking on the bright side: it looked good. This was one handsome slice of gluten-free bread. If you confined yourself to visual observation of a slice, it was a dead ringer for edible bread. And there appeared to be a whole community of gluten-free people online who thought this was the best gluten-free bread, upon whose endorsements we had based our mail order of a whole case of the stuff. But sadly, our best efforts to eat each slice straight out of the toaster proved impossible in the long run. And at about $7 a loaf, plus shipping, it was incompatible with our food budget.

All the while, our family's monthly expenses were growing by leaps and bounds, and we just weren't eating well. None of us felt quite right, but we didn't yet know where to turn.

So out of necessity I began to search, mostly online, for gluten-free recipes that I could make from scratch. At first, I experienced a renaissance of kitchen confidence, but it was inevitably short-lived. Many of the gluten-free recipes I found were full of ingredients that proved obscure and expensive, and the instructions were so complicated that, at times, I felt like I needed a degree in chemistry just to understand them. Did it really have to be so difficult? I started wondering if I couldn't do a better job on my own. After all, I was armed with necessity, the mother of invention.

Feeling otherwise trapped, I committed myself to trying to convert my repertoire of conventional recipes to gluten-free goodness. My first scratch baking attempts were, well, dismal failures. They tasted terrible, not to mention that they were these sad, weepy piles of dough. My cupcakes were crumbling into tiny bits, along with my hopefulness (cue the violins). Finally, I started learning about all-purpose gluten-free flours that, with the addition of a binder called xanthan gum, could substitute cup for cup for conventional wheat flours. After two tries, I finally made a gluten-free carrot cake that looked pretty handsome— and tasted as good as it looked. I was back in business!

After a few more successes, and fewer outright failures, my experiments grew bolder. I began to hone my skills and refine my recipes, making them better and better. Finally, I realized that the sky was the limit—gluten-free or not—and that gluten-free cooking and baking doesn't have to be a daunting challenge when you focus on the right ingredients and have the right instruction.

How to Succeed in Gluten-Free Without Really Trying

I started to realize that, with a few simple tricks, I could reduce my family's grocery bills significantly, something that became more and more important as we felt the effects of the new economy. I went from spending, on average, $175 a week for groceries to spending less than $100 a week. And not only were we eating better, the food seemed more plentiful. Oddly enough, although my husband and I were part of a celiac support group, and even though more and more people we knew were avoiding gluten for one reason or another, the cost of living gluten-free was something that nobody seemed to be talking about—at least not at first. Only when I began to mention how we were saving all this money, always to a surprised and eager audience, did I begin to realize what an important, but under-the-radar, issue this had become. Since everyone wanted to know my secrets, I started a blog called *Gluten-Free on a Shoestring*. In short order, I began to enjoy gluten-free cooking and baking more and more. As both the blog and my collection of recipes grew, I began receiving scores of e-mails from readers, enthusiastic that saving money and living a gluten-free life full of flavor and possibilities were not mutually exclusive after all.

So this book, as a natural extension of the Web site, represents the culmination of many years of hard work, experimentation, and perfection of recipes created in response to the demands of both my family and my readers. You, too, can be in on the secret, and learn to feed yourself, your family, and your guests fabulous gluten-free food—while still keeping an eye on the household budget. Think of how liberating it will be to satisfy your heart's desire in the kitchen, no worries about gluten or about the grocery bill. You'll soon feel freer to entertain, knowing that you can make a tasty, satisfying meal, complete with dessert, for everyone, even the most discriminating foodies.

The recipes in this book are not about making time-consuming, complicated, restaurant-quality food. They're about traditional staples, easy dinners, and comfort foods—the things that we all crave these days (the gluten-free among us even more). This approach will not only save you money but will allow you to feed your family consciously and deliberately—something that we all should do more often. And you'll reap the rewards when you hear your children literally sing while they eat their dinner, as do mine.

This book will also:

· share a whole bunch of strategies for saving money both at the market every week, and in the kitchen every day
· teach you how to build meals around naturally gluten-free foods and how to "piggyback" one dish off of another to save time and money
· show you the basic foods and kitchen equipment that you really need (hint: there's not much) and give you advice on how to stock your kitchen with the ingredients that are the most versatile for gluten-free cooking

There are a few simple skills you can master that will dramatically expand your meal repertoire, and this book will share all of them—there is no need to get bored just because you're on a budget. Together, in this book, we'll make simple but delicious pancakes and blueberry muffins, soft pretzels and wontons, the perfect chocolate chip cookies, and the ultimate in birthday cakes. Step by step, in the plain language of everyday home cooking, I'll show you how to make the comfort foods my family and I love, like chicken pot pie and macaroni and cheese. You'll know how to bake a delicious apple pie when apples are abundant and even make your own fresh pasta—all gluten-free, all deliciously and inexpensively.

I think you'll also be surprised when you learn how easy it is, with the right instruction and a little bit of practice, to make yeast breads, including never-fail white sandwich bread for packing everyone's lunches. Making your own fresh bread is a uniquely joyful experience, and when you settle upon an all-purpose gluten-free flour blend you love, you'll be able to make everything in this book easily and on a budget. There are some who bake with a complicated bevy of exotic gluten-free flours, tweaking a tablespoon here and another sort of flour-I-have-never-heard-of there. When I go down that road, I always end up with remnants of flours in the wrong proportions, followed by a major bout of kitchen shyness, thinking I've lost my touch. Trust me: stick with the basics, and you'll feel more confident and competent, both about your budget and about the way that kitchen of yours hums. You'll be amazed how much more enjoyable life is when you simplify how you cook and how your family eats. Never underestimate the power of kitchen confidence.

Remember: life is sweet and fun. Gluten is expendable.
Warmly,
Nicole

One

Shoestring Strategies:
Saving at the Store and
in Your Kitchen

lthough I was never a spendthrift, saving money wasn't always second nature to me. I was by no means born with a budget mindset, but by necessity, I earned it. So I understand that, until a Shoestring Mentality (to coin a phrase) becomes second nature, it can seem like a chore and even a burden to pay attention to saving money. You may even assume that the savings are not worth the effort. But if you're shopping for gluten-free ingredients, it *is* worth the effort—and that's where this book comes in.

Plain and simple, prepared gluten-free specialty foods are expensive. In fact, the *Canadian Journal of Dietetic Practice and Research* reported that gluten-free foods can cost nearly 250 percent more than conventional foods. If you're newly gluten-free, you're probably still suffering from sticker shock. One day, you're spending a modest $2.50 for a loaf of bread at the supermarket, and the next, you're paying $8.00 or more for a gluten-free version. Or you go from paying $1.99 for a whole box of chocolate chip cookies to paying $7.00 for a tiny package of just six. At first, you may even thank your lucky stars that there are such things on the market these days as a readily available loaf of gluten-free bread or box of cookies, whatever the cost. There can be a real sense of loss when you go gluten-free, and these packaged gluten-free foods may seem like a life raft. It's not that they necessarily taste so terrific (and often they don't), it's just that going gluten-free can seem so overwhelming, and many of us aren't accustomed to making things like a loaf of bread from scratch at home anyhow. The idea of "relearning" how to cook a whole new way can feel like a tall order. So it may seem easier to turn to gluten-free packaged foods, no matter the cost—and that's where your food budget takes an unexpected turn for the worse.

I believe there's a different, and better, way. In this book, I will demystify the process and teach you how to make a big difference in the way you cook and in the way your family eats, with just a modest shift in perspective. You'll be eating fresh, homemade gluten-free foods that warm your home and your heart with a feeling of pride, give you a well-earned sense of accomplishment, and leave you with more money in your pocket at the end of the day. In this chapter, you'll learn a few meal-planning and money-saving strategies, and after that, I'll help you stock your pantry so that a savory and satisfying gluten-free meal for the whole family is at your fingertips every night of the week. Soon you won't need to rely upon a stockpile of overpriced, frozen gluten-free meals and desserts when you feel like you're out of fresh food (or ideas). You really won't run out of either for quite some time.

So let's begin. Here are nine ways you can start saving right away:

Tip #1: Use Coupons

To illustrate how far I've come, you should know that my husband's people are Coupon People. They go way back. Okay, I don't really know how far back they go, but I have firsthand evidence as far back as my father-in-law, and his practice borders on the obsessive. By contrast, for most of my life, I thought that "double coupons" at the market meant that you could use two coupons for the same item at the same time. Reasonable enough, I thought. For the still uninitiated, when a market accepts double coupons, it actually means that they will double your coupons, giving you twice the savings indicated on the coupon. How could I have seen that one coming? If I had, I would have cast the thought aside, assuming it was arrogance to expect such royal treatment.

Coupons are no longer limited only to the Sunday newspaper variety. There are lots of other ways to use coupons to bring your gluten-free budget back down to earth. Here are a few of my secrets:

Online Coupon Sites

Like most things, coupons have evolved with technology. There are sites like **Coupons.com** and **Redplum.com** that allow you to select and print coupons for a variety of mainstream brands. You're not likely to find many gluten-free specialty brands, but you will find many naturally gluten-free products from companies like Green Giant, Smucker's, Smart Balance, Yoplait, and more. On the specialty side of things, there's **Mambosprouts.com.** This is the company that produces those little coupon books that you often find in health food stores and places like Whole Foods Market. Their Web site has printable coupons for many organic and health food brands, which means there's usually some gluten-free products in the mix.

Supermarket Web Sites

Most major supermarkets have areas on their Web sites dedicated to helping you save money. You'll typically find the weekly circular, plus printable coupons from manufacturers and sometimes from the store itself. Some markets even have e-coupons that you can store on your frequent shopper card. Here are the names and links to a handful of supermarket coupon pages:

A & P: http://www.apfreshonline.com/pages_conCenter_CH.asp
Albertson's: http://albertsons.coupons.smartsource.com/smartsource/
index.jsp?Link=3EUL5M4OMDERO
Genuardi's: http://www.genuardis.com/IFL/Grocery/Coupons
Hannaford:
http://www.hannaford.com/coupon_section/Coupons/22222.uts
Kroger: http://www.kroger.com/in_store/Pages/coupon_landing.aspx
Lucky Supermarkets:
http://luckysupermarkets.gsnrecipes.com/storelocator.aspx
Price Chopper: http://www2.pricechopper.com/coupons/
Publix: http://www.publix.com/save/Home.do
Safeway: http://www.safeway.com/IFL/Grocery/Coupons
Smith's: http://www.smithsfoodanddrug.com/Pages/default.aspx

Here are two additional markets that are worthy of special mention:

Earth Fare: http://www.earthfare.com/HealthySavings/Coupons.aspx
Earth Fare calls itself "the healthy supermarket," which is good news for gluten-free shoppers. Their Web site has lots of printable coupons and you'll almost always find a variety of gluten-free products and brands such as Applegate Farms, Pirate's Booty and San-J. And if you register for the store's newsletter, you'll get e-mails with additional in-store coupons, often for things like free eggs, free produce, or money off your next shopping order.

Whole Foods Market: www.wholefoodsmarket.com/coupons
Whole Foods Market is one of the largest natural foods markets around, with locations in about forty U.S. states, Canada, and England. Their Web site has a coupon page that is updated frequently and features many gluten-free products. Visit frequently to find coupons for brands like EnviroKidz, Rice Dream, Blue Diamond, Arrowhead Mills, LÄRABAR, and others. And here's the kicker: thanks to a tip from several readers of the blog, I learned that these Whole Foods coupons are technically store coupons. So if you happen to have a manufacturer's coupon for the same product, they'll let you use both of them. Who knew? Maybe my definition of "double coupons" was right all along!

Company Web Sites

Sometimes the best way to find coupons is to go directly to the source. Visit the Web sites of the companies that make the products you use, and you'll see that many of them have printable coupons right on their Web sites. And be sure to check the sites for a place to register for promotions and discounts. Sometimes I fill out an online comment form and ask if they would be willing to send me some coupons. You'd be surprised how many will oblige.

Here are a few examples of company Web sites that offer coupons:

Arrowhead Mills: http://www.arrowheadmills.com

Blue Bunny (ice cream):
  https://www.bluebunny.com/iScreamTeam/Coupons/Coupons.aspx
Blue Diamond (almond milk, gluten-free crackers, nuts):
  http://www.bluediamond.com/index.cfm?navid=8
Cascadian Farms (frozen fruit and vegetables):
  http://www.cascadianfarm.com/coupons/default.aspx
Crunchmaster (gluten-free crackers):
  http://www.crunchmaster.com/ppccoupon.aspx
Goya: http://www.goya.com/english/coupons.html
Horizon Dairy:
  https://horizonregistration.icmodus.com/default.aspx?bhcp=1
Land O Lakes (great for saving on butter, eggs, cheese):
  http://www.landolakes.com/SimpleRewards/Offers.aspx
Silk Soy Milk: https://silkregistration.icmodus.com/default.aspx?bhcp=1
Stonyfield Farm: http://www.stonyfield.com/register/
Tribe Hummus: http://www.tribehummus.com
Udi's Gluten Free Foods: http://udisglutenfree.com/ppc-gluten-free-udis

Facebook Fan Pages

As more companies recognize the value of social media, they're using sites like Facebook to promote their products, hold contests and, you guessed it, to distribute coupons. Search around to see if your favorite brands have Facebook pages. If you "like" the page, you just might get rewarded with a coupon or free sample.

Tip #2: Practice Once-a-Week Cooking

In the first chapter of recipes (see page 35), I'll introduce you to rudimentary recipes for simple but deliciously pitch-perfect stock, doughs, crusts, sauces, and other basics. To that end, I stock my refrigerator every single week with what I consider the building blocks of a week's worth of tasty gluten-free dinners: **Pizza Dough** (page 44), **Scratch Black Beans** (page 37), **Fresh Gluten-**

free **Pasta Dough** (page 43), **Chicken Stock** (page 35), ground beef cooked with onions and garlic, and cooked brown rice.

To the pizza dough and cooked ground beef, simply add tomato sauce, grated cheese, and chopped frozen broccoli; you'll have a complete meal on the table in less than 30 minutes. The black beans are great for a quick (and super healthy) meal of rice and beans, **Black Bean Hummus** (page 63), or an incredibly flavorful black bean soup when simmered with some **Chicken Stock** (page 35).

You *will* need to commit to cooking—eating gluten-free on the cheap means you'll be cooking from scratch—but you *won't* need to be tethered to the kitchen. Now, I don't like cooking an entire week's worth of dinners and desserts on the weekend, and then sleepwalking through the rest of the week. Relying upon these basics is how I avoid that kind of living. I divide most of my cooking of basics between two separate days of the week, usually Sunday and either Tuesday or Wednesday. That way, my basics are always fresh and accessible. We should enjoy life, not just scrape by. I want my children to develop a healthy relationship with food. Three times a day, every day, we pause . . . and we eat. As long as we live in some measure of good health, we will repeat that pattern every day for the rest of our lives.

Tip #3: Practice Once-a-Month Cooking

In addition to stocking the refrigerator once a week, about once a month I create a few meals that are just one or two steps away from completion. Then I store them in the freezer. For example:

1. I often make **Macaroni-&-Cheese** (page 149) on the stove top, pour it into a 9 x 13-inch baking dish, cover it, and freeze it until I'm ready to use it.
2. I make extra **Potato Gnocchi** (page 126), freeze them in one even layer on a rimmed baking sheet, then place them in a resealable freezer bag and boil them when I'm ready.

3. I shape raw **Chocolate Chip Cookie** dough (page 200) into a cylinder, freeze it, and then I have slice-and-bake cookies whenever I need them.

4. I make and shape **Buttermilk** or **Sweet Potato Biscuits** (pages 100 and 102) and freeze them in a single layer before baking, then bake them when I need them.

5. **Dinner Rolls** (page 98) also turn out very well if you underbake them by a few minutes, freeze them, and then pop them in a hot oven for about 5 to 7 minutes before serving.

Many other recipes lend themselves to being frozen after preparation, but before baking. Examples that you'll find here in *Gluten-Free on a Shoestring* include:

Spinach Pie (page 134)
Beef Potstickers (page 165)
Apple-Cinnamon Toaster Pastries (page 70)
Bagels (page 74)
Berry Scones (page 82)
Cinnamon Rolls (page 76)
Dinner Rolls (page 98)
Graham Crackers (page 214)
Sugar Cookies (page 208)
Chocolate Wafer Cookies (page 212)
Ginger Cookies (page 206)
Apple Pie (page 224)

And remember that breads, like **White Sandwich Bread** (page 104), **Brioche Bread** (page 108), **English Muffin Bread** (page 106), and **French Bread** (page 91) freeze very well after they're baked and cooled—simply defrost the bread overnight in the refrigerator. With nothing more than a well-conceived but flexible routine of cooking and preparation, you can greatly reduce your food budget and spending, eat better gluten-free foods, and enjoy yourself in the process.

Tip #4: "Piggyback" Your Meals

Next, learn to piggyback one meal upon another to make the most of basic ingredients, which in turn allows you to buy loads of whatever happens to be in season and on sale at the market without allowing anything to go to waste. Here of some examples of this idea at work: when you're rolling out pizza dough to make pizza, roll out a little extra for **Beef "Pot Pie"** (page 156). If you're making polenta for **Polenta Pizza** (page 130), make **Tomato Polenta** (page 147). **Lo Mein** (page 154), **Szechuan Meatballs** (page 151), and **Beef Potstickers** (page 165) all go well with **Hoisin Sauce** (page 54). With this in mind, I'll make a double batch of the sauce and serve those three meals in the same week. If you have made 3 or 4 quarts of **Chicken Stock** (page 35), use it in place of water to cook more flavorful brown rice. You can also use it to make **Tortilla Soup** (page 168), **Lemon Chicken** (page 167), **Crispy Asian-Style Tofu** (page 138), **Pot Roast** (page 174), or perhaps some **Tomato Soup** (page 140). When in doubt, wrap something old and commonplace (like chicken breast) in something new and exciting (like **Savory Pastry Crust** [page 41]. Works every time.

I do my best to make at least a loose meal plan each week to take care of weeknight dinners, because it makes my life easier, and it makes meal piggybacking simple to do. Saturdays always seem kind of ad hoc, and since I cook so many basics on Sundays, dinner evolves quite naturally and always has a special dessert, like **Chocolate Sandwich Cookies** (page 205) or a delicious **Apple Pie** (page 192). For example, my week's menu might look like this:

1. **Monday: Tortilla Soup** (page 168) with dinner rolls, **Vanilla Pudding** (page 232) for dessert (pudding made on Sunday and chilled overnight; dinner rolls from my freezer stash, soup simmering in the evening while I get other things done around the house).

2. **Tuesday:** Sliced **Meatlove** (page 162) with **Barbecue Sauce** (page 55) on sliced bread (for example, **White Sandwich Bread** [page 104] or **Brioche Bread** [page 108]) and side salad drizzled with homemade vinaigrette (double recipe of Meatlove made this evening, half frozen for use on Thursday, bread from freezer stock, vinaigrette made on Sunday).

3. **Wednesday:** Black bean and cheese burritos with chopped, defrosted frozen broccoli, served with brown rice (**Scratch Black Beans** [page 37] made on Sunday, **Flour Tortillas** [page 120] made this evening). Defrost rest of raw Meatlove in refrigerator overnight for use on Thursday.

4. **Thursday:** Meatball heroes and tomato sauce on **French Bread** (page 91), with defrosted frozen spinach sautéed in garlic and oil (meatballs made from Meatlove defrosted in the refrigerator overnight, French Bread defrosted from freezer stash and warmed in a 250°F oven, spinach defrosted and sautéed before serving).

5. **Friday:** Who doesn't love pizza?! **Pizza Dough** (page 44) made earlier in the week, rolled out and baked tonight. Topped with defrosted frozen broccoli, defrosted frozen spinach, slices of tomato, and/or browned ground beef and sautéed onions.

Tip #5: Stretch Your Food

If any gluten-free bread (gasp!) goes stale, make **Bread Pudding** (page 81). Bananas browning too quickly? Make **Banana Pancake Muffins** (page 86), or even freeze them whole and unpeeled. Then when you need to use those bananas, just microwave them for about 30 seconds to soften before baking. Potatoes starting to go bad? Make a **Tortilla Española** (page 65). The cupboards seem bare, but you notice you have lots of milk on hand, and you know there's some cornmeal in the back of your pantry. Make **Cornmeal Spoonbread** (page 146) and serve it with some black beans. You just went apple picking, and the apples are starting to show their age. Happens to me all the time, since in the orchard, an extra bag seems like a great idea. It's another story when you get home. Make a quick applesauce by peeling, coring, and slicing the apples, putting them in a heavy-bottom saucepan with sugar and ground cinnamon to taste and a little water to prevent the apples from burning. Even better, make an **Apple Crisp** (page 224), which is nearly just as simple to do as applesauce.

Check the freezer. If you have a lot of frozen spinach, make a quick **Spinach Pie** (page 134) (no excuses—that **Olive Oil Crust** [page 42] doesn't need to rise, so it's ready in a snap). Just poke around your refrigerator, freezer, and pantry. There's plenty there to satisfy everyone.

Tip #6: Be Smart about How You Store Your Food

For example, according to *Prevention* magazine, store onions and potatoes in the refrigerator, but separately, since the moisture in potatoes will cause onions to age faster. They'll last longer, and as an added bonus, those cold onions give off fewer fumes when you cut them. Easier on the wallet, easier on those tender eyes of yours. Store your all-purpose gluten-free flour in an airtight container on your counter or in your pantry, unless you don't plan to use it all in one year's time, in which case you should store it in the refrigerator. If possible, store apples in a separate crisper, away from other foods, since they can rot other foods faster. If you're using reduced-sodium gluten-free soy sauce, store it in the refrigerator because it will spoil faster than its full-sodium counterpart. Store eggs on the bottom shelf, in the container you bought them in, and keep that container closed so the odors of other foods don't mingle with your eggs.

Tip #7: If It's on Sale, Buy in Bulk

When potatoes of any kind are on sale, stock up and make **Oven Hash Brown Quiche** (page 68), **Potato Gnocchi** (page 126), **Potato Bread** (page 112), **Shepherd's Pie** (page 164), and **Tomato Soup** (page 140). When red bell peppers are on sale, buy a bunch, then roast them (see **Roasted Red Peppers**, page 38) and make **Red Pepper Hummus** (page 62) or layer them in a **French Bread** (page 91) sandwich.

In addition to buying some items online (pages 26–29), you can also lower your gluten-free spending by just buying whatever essentials you can find at your regular supermarket. Check the circular that lists store specials from at least one market every week. Certain cooking staples, like unsalted butter quarters and ricotta cheese, are typically on sale pretty often. Be sure to use the store's loyalty or "club" card to get the savings without having to use any coupons. When items like these are on sale, stock up. Just check the sell-by and use-by dates carefully and reach toward the back of the grocer's dairy case for the newest products. Butter frequently has a very long shelf life and can also be frozen and used after the date stamped on the packaging. (Just trust your nose. When dairy is spoiled, it smells spoiled.)

Tip #8: Grow a Vegetable Garden

Even better than smart shopping and buying produce when it's on sale, plant a garden when the weather allows in your climate and grow your own bell peppers. Whatever the climate, with few exceptions, growing your own vegetables can be a very smart way to defray the high cost of buying produce.

But even so, there are some vegetables like carrots and celery that are so inexpensive to buy fresh in the market that I do not ever grow my own. Then there are those vegetables that are far superior when grown fresh and thrive so readily that it's silly not to try your hand at growing your own. Tomatoes, zucchini, and cucumbers come to mind. Speaking of cucumbers, why is it that, even in the middle of the summer where I live, I can't remember the last time I saw a cucumber on sale for less than 50¢ *each?* I'm thinking about opening up a small farm stand in front of my house. In my spare time. Fifty cents for one cucumber is highway robbery!

Tip #9: Buy Frozen Veggies

Don't worry. If the very thought of growing your own vegetables is making your palms sweat, don't let it slow you down. Forget the garden. During most of the year, I use frozen vegetables. They're frozen at the peak of freshness and typically cost heaps less than their fresh counterparts. A 1-pound bag of good-quality frozen broccoli crowns runs me less than $2.00 and there is no waste. One pound of fresh broccoli, on sale, will cost at least $1.75, it takes up a ton of space in my refrigerator, and preparing it is much more labor intensive. Frozen vegetables are ready whenever and in whatever quantity you need them, and they don't spoil for ages. Use frozen, buy fresh when it's on sale, and keep on keepin' on.

Two

What to Buy
and from Where

Buying whole foods, gluten-free or not, can be expensive—but it doesn't have to be if you follow a few straightforward guidelines. In the recipes in this book, I will walk you through how to make good use of whole-food ingredients to create delicious, satisfying foods that everyone will love. But first things first.

We'll start with the proper contents of a well-stocked, gluten-free pantry, the backbone of your kitchen. These are the items that you're bound to use on a regular basis, so it's always money well spent. You don't have to buy them every week. You just have to keep them in stock, because they make everything else possible. Then we'll go through what to buy at the market and online on a regular basis. Finally, we'll review the basic kitchen equipment that you'll need (hint: it isn't much). Think of these everyday basics like good, clean underwear. You wouldn't carefully select a beautiful outfit to wear (here, a great recipe), one that makes you feel like a million bucks, only to throw on a pair of granny pants that give you unsightly panty lines and keep you tugging at them all night, would you? Of course not. Carefully select just the right basic food items, and you can rock any recipe in your kitchen.

Our pantry items in place, we'll move on to clever strategies for choosing which perishable foods to buy every week, and for getting the most out of your weekly trip to the market.

The Well-Stocked, Gluten-Free, Shoestring-Friendly Pantry

Do you know any home cooks who seem to "throw together" a dinner with what seems like little to no planning? Cooks who can effortlessly accommodate a few more guests at the last minute without simply adding some more water to thin the soup? These cooks know how to keep their pantries well stocked, and they're confident in their own kitchens. This can be you! Updating your pantry with essential, all-purpose items is your first step toward the good, gluten-free life, and it's within reach.

When you always have what you need to prepare meals on hand (and don't have to reinvent the wheel every time you need to write a shopping list), you'll be much less tempted to order take-out, rely on frozen gluten-free pizzas, or grab those pricey packages of gluten-free cupcakes. In my kitchen, I don't stock store-bought sauces and dressings. Instead, I stock the ingredients that serve as the bases for those sauces and dressings. I don't stock ready-made pie shells, but I do stock the ingredients I need to make basic sweet and savory pie crusts. Then I make some of the dough of each and freeze it in portions. I always have the ingredients on hand to make last-minute cupcakes and frosting ("I forgot to tell you there's a birthday party in school tomorrow, Mom!") and perfect chocolate chip cookies. I even make my own slice-and-bake cookie dough, shaped into a log and frozen for just such an emergency.

Now, let's take a look at what you should expect to buy on a regular basis. The following items are the ingredients that should have a constant presence in your cupboard, refrigerator, and freezer, as the case may be. Many of you may already have most of these items right now and just need to supplement with a few more to round things out. If you don't have many of these staples, you will have to stock up, and there will be an up-front cost. But this is an investment, as essential to the proper functioning of your kitchen as the sink and your stove. And like any good investment, over time, it will pay off—day after day, meal after meal. Count on it.

Pantry Staples

Oil, Vinegar, and Condiments

- ☐ Extra-virgin olive oil
- ☐ Canola oil (or other neutral vegetable oil)
- ☐ Sesame oil
- ☐ Nonstick cooking spray (most are gluten-free, but be a savvy consumer)
- ☐ White wine vinegar
- ☐ Balsamic vinegar (regular or white)
- ☐ Apple cider vinegar
- ☐ Rice vinegar
- ☐ Gluten-free soy sauce (like La Choy)
- ☐ Worcestershire sauce (check to make sure the brand is gluten-free)

Grocery

- ☐ Tomato paste (canned or in a tube)
- ☐ Whole peeled tomatoes (canned)
- ☐ Tomato sauce (canned)
- ☐ Honey
- ☐ Unsulphured molasses
- ☐ Pure maple syrup
- ☐ Peanut butter
- ☐ Mayonnaise
- ☐ Tahini (sesame paste)

Beans, Pasta, and Grains

- ☐ Dried black beans
- ☐ Dried gluten-free pasta
- ☐ Gluten-free rolled oats (only buy certified gluten-free)
- ☐ Brown rice
- ☐ Short-grain rice (like Arborio rice)
- ☐ Coarsely ground (yellow) cornmeal
- ☐ Precooked cornmeal
- ☐ Quinoa flakes
- ☐ Gluten-free cornflake cereal

Baking

- ☐ All-purpose gluten-free flour
- ☐ Xanthan gum
- ☐ Cornstarch
- ☐ Baking powder
- ☐ Baking soda
- ☐ Active dry yeast
- ☐ Brown sugar (light or dark)
- ☐ Confectioner's sugar
- ☐ Granulated sugar
- ☐ Unsweetened (Dutch-processed) cocoa powder
- ☐ Semi-sweet chocolate chips
- ☐ Light coconut milk (canned)
- ☐ Low-fat evaporated milk
- ☐ Cream of tartar
- ☐ Vegetable shortening
- ☐ Pure vanilla extract
- ☐ Whole vanilla beans

Seasonings

- ☐ Kosher salt
- ☐ Table (fine) salt
- ☐ Black peppercorns (for grinding)
- ☐ Ground cinnamon
- ☐ Dried oregano
- ☐ Dried parsley
- ☐ Ground cumin
- ☐ Chile flakes
- ☐ Chile powder
- ☐ Dried bay leaves

Fruits and Nuts

- ☐ Whole cranberries
- ☐ Dried cranberries (unsweetened)

☐ Thompson raisins
☐ Sliced almonds
☐ Pecan pieces

Frozen Vegetables
☐ Frozen peas
☐ Frozen broccoli crowns
☐ Frozen spinach (chopped or whole)
☐ Frozen corn kernels

To Market, to Market:
What to Buy Weekly at the Grocery

Now that you have your pantry shopping list, here's a meal shopping list for a typical week cooking the *Gluten-Free on a Shoestring* way. Of course, this is a general list, and you can adapt it easily to accommodate any other dietary needs and restrictions you adhere to.

Your Weekly Ingredient Shopping List
(remember your regular pantry items are not included here)

Fresh Fruits and Vegetables
☐ Bananas
☐ Apples (Granny Smith, Golden Delicious, McIntosh, etc., especially in the fall when they're cheaper)
☐ Whole carrots
☐ Celery hearts
☐ Leeks
☐ Potatoes (red-skin, yellow-skin, selecting potatoes of similar size to one another for even cooking)
☐ Yellow onions
☐ Garlic
☐ Ginger root

- ☐ Butternut squash
- ☐ Sweet potatoes
- ☐ Lemons

Dairy Case
- ☐ Extra-large eggs
- ☐ Mozzarella cheese (or nondairy cheese)
- ☐ Cheddar cheese (or nondairy cheese)
- ☐ Part-skim ricotta cheese
- ☐ Unsalted butter (or nondairy, trans fat–free margarine)
- ☐ Low-fat milk (or nondairy milk, such as soy milk, nut milk, or rice milk)
- ☐ Extra-firm tofu

Meat
- ☐ Bone-in, skin-on chicken thighs
- ☐ Bone-in, skin-on chicken breasts
- ☐ Skinless boneless chicken breasts
- ☐ Lean ground beef

Now on to a few bits of advice about some foods used in these recipes:

Tomato sauce. You'll notice that there is no recipe for tomato sauce in this book. I found that it simply wasn't economical to make, since one can buy a 28-ounce can of high-quality prepared tomato sauce for less than $2. I was using cans of whole peeled tomatoes to make my own sauce, and that requires me to simmer the sauce so it will reduce, which was costing me more money, for less sauce. It just didn't make sense, gluten or no gluten.

Eggs. All of the recipes in this book that call for eggs specify extra-large eggs. That's because gluten-free flours tend to require more moisture than conventional flours, and extra-large eggs are very handy in providing that moisture. Although they are marginally more expensive than large eggs, here the small added cost is worth it.

Cheese. I often buy certain cheeses, such as Parmesan, in blocks and grate as I go. With other cheeses, like mozzarella, I often buy them already grated (note that, as with anything already prepared and packaged, carefully check labels and ingredients to ensure that the product is gluten-free). Although my general rule is not to pay someone else to do something that you could do easily for yourself, this is a notable exception. Buying grated cheese is frequently less expensive than buying a block of cheese, believe it or not. Plus, a package of grated cheese has a longer life in your refrigerator than a block of cheese does. And there is nothing more expensive than spoiled food that must be disposed of.

Fresh fruits and vegetables. The same rule of thumb applies to fresh produce, especially fruit. I look at it this way: if I know that fruit is going to be eaten within a week, I am happy to go out of my way to a produce-only market that sells fruits and vegetables that are a few days old and much less expensive. But if there's a chance that it won't all be eaten in a week or less, it is more cost-effective to spend a bit more on the very freshest produce, if it is available where you live. If you do buy produce that has aged a few days, be sure to buy only what you know you will use straight away. Remember the rule about spoiled food: if you end up having to throw it away, you haven't saved anything.

Buy bananas that are bright yellow with a hint of green, and try to buy them in a place that sells them by the banana, not by weight. You'll find it's a better deal—and you can pick the largest bananas from the bunch.

Buy the produce that is currently in season. These days, if you are able to shop in a large market, you will find all fruits all year round. But in the case of off-season produce, like berries in the winter, what you'll find will be almost universally much more expensive and much less tasty. Wait to buy stone fruit like peaches, plums, and nectarines in the late summer, stock up on apples in the fall and berries all summer, and you won't be sorry. There are some exceptions, like grapes that are flown in from all around the world and are good quality all year (and are always on sale somewhere) and hothouse tomatoes that are always good (but only buy them on sale or they'll be way too expensive). Start turning your attention to what seems plentiful during a particular season, and you'll be glad you did.

Dairy items. Only in a real pinch should you have to pay full price for mainstream market items like butter, cheese, and milk, since they so regularly go on sale. When milk is on sale, it is often a "loss-leader," so the store may actually be selling it below cost to lure you into the store with the hope that you'll buy other items at full price (which, of course, we don't plan to do, but they don't know that).

Meat. Meats also tend to go on sale at the market pretty regularly, and often at a steep discount. Buy extra and freeze what you can't use right away. Buy larger "family packs" of meat, unwrap the package at home, use what you can right away, and freeze the rest in airtight packaging. Just like the grocer does, rotate perishable items in your refrigerator, making sure the freshest foods are on top and easily within reach.

Ordering Online

Many people say that if you have to eat gluten-free, now is the best time to do so. In recent years the number, and availability, of gluten-free products has expanded dramatically. Everyday supermarkets now carry all-purpose gluten-free flours, and some even have dedicated natural or organic food sections with gluten-free products. There are also stores like Trader Joe's and Whole Foods that carry a nice selection of gluten-free products. That's the good news. But not everyone has access to these stores. Generally speaking, online retailers still offer a much broader selection of gluten-free products and ingredients. Plus, if you're smart about the way you order online, you can stretch your gluten-free budget. Here are a few ideas.

1. Order Your All-Purpose Gluten-Free Flour Online

As I mentioned, you can find certain brands of all-purpose gluten-free flour in many supermarkets and specialty stores. But remember, you're going to be using a lot of gluten-free flour, so buying it in 1-pound, retail-size bags is not very shoestring-friendly. You need a better solution.

Over the years, I have used many brands of all-purpose gluten-free flour, and I have finally settled on Better Batter Gluten Free Flour (www.betterbatter.org). Better Batter works very well in any gluten-free recipe I have tried. The ingredients as listed are rice flour, brown rice flour, potato starch, potato flour, pectin (lemon derivative), and xanthan gum. Those of you who have other food allergies and sensitivities, though, take note: the packaging warns that the product is processed on equipment that also processes dairy, eggs, soy, and tree nuts. There are many things that really make this brand stand out. For starters, as noted above, the flour blend already incorporates xanthan gum, which happens to be one of the more expensive gluten-free baking ingredients. Score. (Just be sure to omit the xanthan gum ingredient from the recipes in this book if you are using Better Batter, or any other all purpose gluten-free flour blend that contains xanthan gum as part of the premade blend.) On top of that, you can order Better Batter in bulk, including 25-pound bags, at a reduced rate. Best of all, the company typically offers reasonable shipping rates. This last point is especially important. If you've ever ordered heavy items like flour or mixes online, you know how those shipping charges can really add up. So when you do the math, Better Batter is a winner.

If you like working with Bob's Red Mill products, check out their Web site (www.bobsredmill.com). You can order a wide range of products from flours and gluten-free oats to cornmeal and yeast, some in bulk sizes, directly from the company. They also post monthly specials online.

2. Save with Amazon.com

Amazon.com? The place to buy books and CDs, right? Yes, that Amazon.com. I love Amazon.com for gluten-free shopping, and there are several reasons why I think you will, too.

You might be surprised to learn that Amazon.com carries many gluten-free items, including well-known brands like Tinkyada Rice Pasta, Arrowhead Mills, Bob's Red Mill Natural Foods, Erewhon Natural Foods, Nature's Path Organic (including EnviroKidz Organic), Amy's Kitchen, Annie's Homegrown, Glutino, and many more. Prices are generally very good and items are often sold in money-saving multipacks. We like multipacks. Also, the majority of Amazon items qualify for free shipping with a minimum purchase of just $25. This is a huge advantage over many specialty gluten-free online retailers.

On top of the good prices and the free shipping, certain Amazon.com products also qualify for the Subscribe & Save Program. This "subscription" service works like this: you sign up and agree to get repeat shipments of your item at a monthly interval you choose. When you do, you get 15 percent off the initial order and all the subsequent ones. The best part is, you can suspend or cancel the subscription at any time, and you will still get the 15 percent off your original order.

Here are a few examples of how shopping at Amazon.com can be a whole lot smarter than your local health food store when it comes to items you use often: one 44-ounce bag of Bob's Red Mill All Purpose GF Flour (sold in a 4-pack) will set you back about $6.40 at Amazon.com. Use the Subscribe & Save Program, and the price drops to about $5.40. I've seen that same bag of flour at health food stores for $8.99. So buying that bag of flour at Amazon.com with Subscribe & Save can, in fact, save you up to 40 percent. Another good example is gluten-free cereal. Take a 10-ounce box of gluten-free Erewhon Crispy Brown Rice (sold in a 6-pack): on Amazon.com, it costs about $3.25; with Subscribe & Save, the price goes down to about $2.75 a box. That same cereal in a health food store can cost $5.00 or more per box. So Amazon.com can save you up to 45 percent. Especially when we're talking about staples like flour and cereal, savings like these add up in a hurry. Give Amazon.com a try, and you'll quickly find that it can save you money on many other kinds of gluten-free staples, like pasta, cornmeal, xanthan gum, and more.

Amazon.com also runs specials on many gluten-free products. At roughly the beginning of every month, they post a number of sales in their "Grocery & Gourmet Food" department. Go to the main page for that department, and then click the "Special Offers" link along the top. If you check regularly, you're sure to stumble upon great discounts on things like Bob's Red Mill products, LÄRABARs, Tinkyada Rice Pasta, gluten-free cereal, among others. One more thing: once you order from Amazon, there's a good chance you'll get e-mails alerting you to some of these specials. Their sales are worth the extra e-mail traffic in your inbox.

3. Sign Up for E-mail Alerts and Newsletters

For selection, you can't beat online retailers like Glutenfree.com and Glutenfree Mall (www.glutenfreemall.com). Visit these sites and sign up for their free e-mail alerts. Again, if you don't mind getting some extra e-mail, it's worth it.

You'll probably receive special offers and discount codes, often for 10 percent off your order. I usually find something of value.

The Best Gluten-Free Values and the Best Places to Find Them

We've talked about plenty of tips for cutting the cost of eating gluten-free. Before I push you out of the nest where you'll be shopping all by yourself, turn the page for a little cheat sheet for reference.

Remember, when you shop smart, you really can extend your food budget. And these savings can go a long way toward offsetting the pain of the extra money we simply must spend on certain gluten-free staples, such as gluten-free dried pasta and all-purpose gluten-free flour (which are typically more expensive than the gluten-containing varieties).

Essential Kitchen Equipment

Finally, let's discuss the equipment you'll need to keep things humming along nicely. A well-equipped kitchen by my standards is one that has an oven in working order, an oven thermometer (most ovens are improperly calibrated and the temperatures are off by quite a lot, so let an oven thermometer be your guide), a stove top with at least one or two burners in working order, a refrigerator, a sink, and some counter space. It doesn't take much. There are, however, a few pieces of equipment that I consider to be money well spent if not entirely essential to a well-appointed kitchen. Remember, you are going to be cooking all of your family's food in this kitchen of yours, and you'll be saving boatloads of money in the process. You should have what you need to do it right.

Kitchen Equipment

1. Oven thermometer (so important to proper functioning it bears repeating) (average cost $15 or less)

BUY ONLINE

(e.g.: Amazon.com, betterbatter.org, bobsredmill.com)

1. Gluten-free flour
2. Gluten-free pasta
3. Gluten-free cereal
4. Corn meal
5. Xanthan gum
6. Certified gluten-free oats

BUY AT THE SUPERMARKET

(on sale and with coupons)

1. Raw meat and chicken
2. Milk and cream
3. Butter
4. Eggs
5. Cheese
6. Dried beans
7. Rice
8. Tomato sauce
9. Produce and frozen vegetables

BUY AT A WAREHOUSE CLUB

(Costco, Sam's Club, BJ's Wholesale)

1. Baking staples (like all types of sugar, baking chips, honey, molasses, kosher salt)
3. Produce, when possible (it's usually very fresh, so it keeps well)
4. Olive oil, vinegars, gluten-free soy sauce, Worcestershire sauce
5. Dried herbs and spices
6. Rice and dry beans, when possible

2. Rimmed metal baking sheets (quarter-sheet and half-sheet pans are particularly useful and fit in most any oven)

3. 10-inch or 12-inch nonstick frying pan

4. Large (7½ quart) enamel cast-iron Dutch oven (I have a Le Creuset, admittedly expensive, but I'm not too proud to tell you that I couldn't love it any more if it were my own flesh and blood. The French know their enameled cast-iron cookware, and it's hard for me to imagine that anything else can come close for performance and heirloom quality. It will cook anything you throw in it with aplomb. It heats quickly and evenly, despite the high performance burners on my stove that tend toward the overzealous. And even stuck-on foods come off easily when you soak it in hot water and soap and then use Barkeeper's Friend, a mild abrasive cleanser that is very similar to Bon Ami. I swear food tastes better when I cook it in my Le Creuset.)

5. Large pasta pot (plus a dedicated colander, if you use one—I don't, since I'm too lazy to clean and dry it every time. Colanders are so hard to dry.)

6. Medium heavy-bottom saucepan (I have a stainless steel Cuisinart brand, and it wasn't cheap [about $75 at a Cuisinart outlet], but it's worth the money for its even cooking and easy cleanup.)

7. Springform pan (no need to spend much on this item)

8. Stand mixer (buy one that will be a workhorse for you and still stand the test of time.)

9. Food processor (indispensable for making things like homemade hummus possible, for grating or slicing large quantities of vegetables, grinding whole cuts of meat. A serviceable machine should cost you no more than $150.)

10. Immersion blender (an inexpensive item—read: don't pay more than $30, give or take—that will earn its keep in just a few uses)

11. Asian-style spider strainer (cheap-o)

12. Wooden cutting board (be sure never to use for anything gluten-containing, as it's porous)

13. Chef's knife or santoku knife (I have a Wusthof Classic 7-inch santoku knife, which is a great all-purpose knife, and I like the way it feels in my hand. It cost about $85, and I bought it years ago and sharpen it somewhat

regularly. If you're having trouble deciding which style and which brand to buy, try going to a chef's store or the knife department of a large department store and speak to a salesperson. They're very knowledgeable.)

14. Serrated carving knife (I have a Wusthof, but for no particular reason. This won't be used nearly as much as your all purpose chef's or santoku knife, so you don't need to break the bank on it, but for slicing all those loaves of gluten-free bread you're going to be turning out, nothing else comes close to a large serrated carving knife.)

15. Small paring knife (I have both a Zyliss and a Wusthof. Neither was very expensive, and it needn't be, but you need this type of knife.)

16. High heat–resistant nylon or silicone large flat nonstick spatula (please, no plastic or it will melt, no metal or it will scratch everything)

17. High high–resistant nylon or silicone slotted spatula (again, no plastic, no metal, please)

18. Vegetable peeler (any will do)

19. Pastry brush (I have a silicone one because I like that it's heat resistant.)

20. Measuring spoons and cups (any will do)

21. Wooden or silicone spoons (silicone will keep very, very well)

22. Silicone whisk (because it's kind to the bottoms of your pots)

23. Rolling pin (I like the French kind, without handles, which just seem to spin and spin.)

A word about keeping your kitchen free of contamination of your gluten-free foods with any foods you have that contain gluten: don't make your life any harder than it has to be. Each time I hear a tale of a household cooking one meal for the only celiac in the family, and one for everyone else in the family, either out of fear that the gluten-free food is not going to be palatable to the nonceliacs, or because of the excessive cost of the gluten-free meal, I shed one sad, lonely tear. Make delicious, reasonably priced gluten-free food, make a lot of it, and invite the neighbors over. Go ahead, host Thanksgiving. I promise you, your family and your guests won't know the difference (except that maybe it'll be better than last year's). To the extent that you must cook and bake any conventional, gluten-containing foods, be careful. Gluten is sticky. Use a dedicated colander for gluten-free pastas and don't even consider using a strainer that has seen the likes of gluten in its lifetime. Put everything you can in the dishwasher, and, when you're preparing, cooking, baking, or serving gluten-free foods, avoid using anything porous (like wood or plastic utensils, cutting boards, or storage containers) that once contained or was used to prepare gluten-containing foods. Exercise caution when reusing basically anything that has lots of grooves and crevices that tend to hold onto crumbs, like nonstick muffin tins and springform pans. That advice about only cooking and baking gluten-free is starting to look better and better, right?

If You're Dairy-Free, Too

On the blog, I get lots of questions about whether dairy-free substitutions can be made in recipes, and the answer is almost always "yes." Every recipe in this book that calls for a dairy-containing ingredient can handle a dairy-free substitute, except where specifically noted otherwise. And the vast majority handle the substitution very well. In my house, we were dairy-free for a spell a few years ago, and we did it for long enough that I did develop some allegiance to specific brands of two particular products: cheese and a butter alternative.

After trying what seemed like scores of dairy-free, gluten-free cheeses, the one that won my heart was, well, Follow Your Heart brand Vegan Gourmet cheese alternatives. It not only says that it melts, but it does, in fact, melt. Sure, it melts a bit better in the microwave than in the oven, but it's simple enough to work around a little quirk like that. It comes in a block, and it even grates nicely.

My choice for a gluten-free, dairy-free butter alternative is Earth Balance brand vegan buttery spread and butter sticks. They're made entirely of nonhydrogenated oils, so they're really nothing like margarine. The sticks can't be beat for cooking and baking, since they are marked, like butter, in tablespoons, making a one-for-one substitution a piece of gluten-free cake.

In all the other dairy alternative product categories, like milk and sour cream, they all seem to work just fine. It's really a matter of taste.

Three

Kitchen Confidence: Basic Recipes That Serve as the Foundation for Many Others

MEAL INGREDIENTS

Chicken Stock

MAKES 2 QUARTS (OR 8 CUPS)

This is a big one. The recipes in this book are awash in Chicken Stock as an ingredient. Where I live, it's common to find prepared gluten-free chicken stock on the shelf of even the smaller grocery chains, and I used to buy it frequently. It's good quality, and it's so handy and versatile. But I tended to be very stingy with it when I shelled out upwards of $2.50 for a mere quart. When I make it myself, my family and I eat the chicken and all of the vegetables we cooked to make the broth, so it's like we're getting the stock for free. And if I leave the vegetables in the stock, and just remove the chicken and the bay leaf, and puree with an immersion blender, it's a wonderfully rich base for **Chicken and Dumplings** (page 170).

4 skin-on, bone-in chicken thighs

2 carrots, cut into 1-inch chunks

2 stalks of celery, cut into 1-inch chunks

1 large yellow onion, peeled and quartered

6 to 8 cloves of garlic, whole with skin removed

1 butternut squash, peeled, seeded, and cut into large chunks

1 dried bay leaf

2 tablespoons kosher salt

1 teaspoon freshly ground black pepper

1. Place the chicken, carrots, celery, onion, garlic, squash, bay leaf, salt, and pepper into a large stockpot. Pour in just enough water to cover the chicken and vegetables.

2. Cover the pot (with the lid tipped a bit) and bring the liquid to a boil. Reduce the heat to medium low and simmer for about 1½ hours, until the chicken is cooked through and the mixture is very fragrant. Remove the chicken and vegetables from the pot, and pour the liquid through a strainer. On the other side of the strainer should be about 2 quarts of Chicken Stock.

Scratch Black Beans

MAKES ABOUT 6 CUPS COOKED BLACK BEANS

These beans are wonderful for rice and beans, can easily be turned into black bean soup, or be rolled up into tortillas with some cheese and salsa for a quick burrito. They are a Shoestring staple. For a vegetarian version of these beans, replace the bacon with 2 to 3 tablespoons of extra-virgin olive oil and 1 teaspoon of kosher salt, and proceed with the rest of the recipe as directed. They will still be remarkably flavorful and versatile. This recipe also works well for dried pinto beans, dried black-eyed peas, and dried small red beans (as distinct from kidney beans, which are larger). They all take about the same amount of time to cook using this method.

¼ pound bacon (about 4 to 6 slices), diced

2 medium (or 1 large) yellow onion(s), chopped

6 cloves garlic, minced

1 pound (16 ounces) dried black beans, rinsed

7 to 8 cups water

2 tablespoons balsamic vinegar

2 tablespoons gluten-free soy sauce (I like La Choy Lite)

1. In a large stockpot, cook the bacon over medium-high heat, stirring occasionally, until most of the fat is rendered from it, about 5 minutes. Add the onions to the pot and sauté them in the bacon fat until the onion is translucent, about 6 minutes. Add the garlic and sauté until fragrant, about 2 minutes.

2. Add the dried black beans to the pot, tossing with the other ingredients to coat. Add the water and simmer, covered, for about 2 hours, or until the beans reach the desired consistency. Check the pot from time to time and add more water if necessary. The beans will absorb more water as they stand after cooking, so you need not be concerned with boiling off the water, but rather with softening the beans to the desired tenderness.

3. Once the beans are cooked to your satisfaction, add the balsamic vinegar and soy sauce, and cook uncovered for 3 to 5 minutes to allow the flavors to come together.

Roasted Red Peppers

MAKES 2 ROASTED RED PEPPERS

It's super simple to roast sweet peppers, and they keep for ages if you pack them in oil. Whenever bell peppers are well priced in your local market, buy a bunch and roast them. They're great in salads, on sandwiches, and they make a beautiful **Roasted Red Pepper Hummus** (page 62). Once roasted, they can be stored either in the refrigerator in olive oil or frozen for later use.

2 large sweet (red) peppers
2 to 4 tablespoons vegetable oil

1. Preheat your oven to 500°F or turn on your oven's broiler (either way will work fine). Line a baking sheet with aluminum foil, brush the foil with some oil, and set the baking sheet aside.

2. Wash the peppers and coat all sides of them with the vegetable oil. Place the peppers on the prepared baking sheet and place it inside the preheated oven, about 6 inches from the top. Once the tops of the peppers begin to blacken (about 5 to 7 minutes), turn them over with tongs and allow the other side to blacken (about another 5 minutes).

3. Once both sides of the peppers are somewhat blackened, remove them from the oven and place them directly into a large bowl. Quickly cover the bowl tightly with plastic wrap to trap the heat inside the bowl. After about 15 to 20 minutes, the heat will have steamed loose the skin of the peppers. Remove the peppers from the bowl, remove the stems, ease the skin off the peppers, slice them open, and scrape out the seeds. If you're not planning to use the peppers right away, you can pack them in an airtight container and cover them in olive oil so they don't dry out.

DOUGHS AND CRUSTS

Sweet Pastry Crust

MAKES ENOUGH CRUST TO MAKE TWO 9-INCH ROUNDS,
EACH WITH AN APPROXIMATE 1-INCH OVERHANG

This recipe yields enough dough to make the top and bottom crusts of a full-size pie. I always make the whole recipe and then freeze whatever I don't need right away, if any. This crust freezes nicely, and it's fabulous for tarts and mini pies, too. In a pinch it can even be used in place of savory crust (oh, live a little!).

2¼ cups all-purpose gluten-free flour

1 teaspoon xanthan gum

½ teaspoon kosher salt

½ teaspoon baking powder

½ cup confectioner's sugar

10 tablespoons unsalted butter, diced and chilled

½ to ¾ cup water, iced (the ice cubes don't count in the volume measurement)

1. In a large bowl, mix the flour, xanthan gum, salt, baking powder, and confectioner's sugar until well combined.

2. Add the cold, diced butter to the bowl of dry ingredients. If you have a pastry blender, cut in the butter by holding on to the handle and pressing the tines of the blender into the mixture over and over again until the mixture resembles small pea-size chunks of butter wrapped in the flour mixture. If you are using two knives, just cross them and cut repeatedly into the mixture until the mixture arrives at small chunks of butter wrapped in the flour mixture. This way, when the small pieces of cold butter are distributed throughout the pastry, surrounded by flour, they expand in the oven and make light and flaky pastry.

3. Add ½ cup ice water to the mixture by the tablespoon. Place plastic sandwich bags on your hands (the old-school, fold-over kind, not the zipper bags)

and squeeze the mixture together tightly in your fists. If the mixture does not hold together, take off the plastic bags, add more water by the tablespoon and squeeze again until you are able to form a respectable ball with your hands. You want to try to handle the dough as little as possible, within reason, to avoid melting the butter with the warmth of your hands.

4. Once you have created a ball, break it in two, and wrap each section separately in plastic wrap and place in the refrigerator. Chill for at least 30 minutes, or as long as overnight, before rolling out and using as you wish.

Shoestring Savings

Savory Pastry Crust

On a shoestring: $1.25 per crust

If you bought it: $3.00 per crust (frozen)

Savory Pastry Crust

MAKES ENOUGH CRUST FOR TWO 9-INCH ROUNDS,
EACH WITH AN APPROXIMATE 1-INCH OVERHANG

Like its sweet cousin, this recipe for savory pastry crust makes enough for the top and bottom of a savory pie or quiche. Without baking powder or baking soda, this crust relies only upon the diced butter that expands as the dough bakes, so it's super important that the butter is cold before making the crust and that you use ice water, not just cold tap water. This is one of those basics that will serve you well—and help you breeze through other recipes, like **Chicken en Croute** (page 160).

2¼ cups all-purpose gluten-free flour
1 teaspoon xanthan gum
½ teaspoon kosher salt
1 stick plus 2 tablespoons (10 tablespoons) unsalted butter, diced and chilled
½ to ¾ cup water, iced (the ice cubes don't count in the volume measurement)

1. In a large bowl, mix the flour, xanthan gum, and salt, until well combined.

2. Add the cold, diced butter to the bowl of dry ingredients. Cut in the butter with a pastry blender if you have one, or just use two knives to cut repeatedly into the mixture. Stop when the mixture resembles small, pea-size chunks of butter wrapped in flour.

3. Add ½ cup ice-cold water to the mixture by the tablespoon. Using plastic sandwich bags as gloves (fancy, I know), squeeze the mixture together tightly in your fists. If it does not hold together, add more water by the tablespoon and squeeze again until you are able to form a respectable ball with your hands. Remember to handle the dough as little as possible so the butter stays cold and evenly distributed.

4. Once you have created a ball, break it in two, and wrap each section separately in plastic wrap and place in the refrigerator. Chill for at least 30 minutes, or as long as overnight, before using.

Savory Olive Oil Crust

MAKES ENOUGH DOUGH FOR A TOP AND BOTTOM CRUST FOR A 9-INCH PIE

It's the olive oil that makes this crust so pliable and makes it brown so beauti-fully. Olive oil is a rich and flavorful oil, though, so although this crust won't marry well with just any combination of ingredients, it will make a crispy and flaky spinach pie. In fact, it makes a wonderful crust for nearly any quiche. And since it does not need any yeast, it's ready in a jiffy.

2 cups all-purpose gluten-free flour
1 teaspoon xanthan gum
1 teaspoon kosher salt
5 tablespoons extra-virgin olive oil
1½ teaspoons white wine vinegar
½ to ¾ cup cold water

1. In a large bowl, add the flour, xanthan gum, and salt and whisk to combine. Pour in the olive oil and white vinegar, and stir with a fork to combine. Add ½ cup of cold water and stir until the flour absorbs the water, then mix or knead until the dough comes together. If the dough is crumbly, add more water by the tablespoon, mixing after each addition, until the dough is smooth.

2. Cover the dough with plastic wrap and place it in the refrigerator to chill for at least 30 minutes. After the dough has chilled, place it between two pieces of plastic wrap and roll until it is about ⅛ inch thick. Once you have rolled the dough, remove one piece of plastic wrap and dust the dough lightly with extra flour, and replace the plastic wrap. Repeat with the other side of the dough. It is now ready to be used for a savory tart or pie.

Fresh Gluten-Free Pasta Dough

MAKES ENOUGH DOUGH TO MAKE ABOUT 12 INDIVIDUAL 1½-INCH SQUARE RAVIOLI

Use this dough to make ravioli, lasagna noodles, cannelloni, linguini, or any other shape you like. With so many dried gluten-free pastas readily available at good prices these days, I tend to use this fresh pasta dough for dishes like **Spinach and Cheese Ravioli** (page 132), which are less readily available in gluten-free varieties and much, much more expensive.

2 cups all-purpose gluten-free flour

1 teaspoon xanthan gum

½ teaspoon kosher salt

1 extra-large egg, at room temperature

1 tablespoon unsalted butter, at room temperature

2 tablespoons extra-virgin olive oil

½ to ⅔ cup warm water, about 100°F

1. In food processor or stand mixer, mix the flour, xanthan gum, salt, egg, butter, and olive oil until well blended. Allow the food processor or mixer to keep blending for a couple of minutes in order to activate the xanthan gum.

2. After blending for a couple minutes, add the water in a slow, steady stream while the machine is on until the mixture comes together in a ball. The dough should be very stiff.

3. Divide the dough into four balls. Roll out each ball of dough between two sheets of plastic wrap until it's about ⅛ inch thick (about the thickness of a nickel). You don't want it to be too thin or it will fall apart when you boil it. If it's too thick, it will be gummy.

Pizza Dough

MAKES CRUST FOR TWO 12-INCH PIZZAS

Pizza dough is one of the single most important staples to have in your kitchen. It is exceedingly simple to make, freezes fantastically well, and then defrosts readily. It even keeps quite well in the refrigerator for a few days after you make it. If you make pizza dough at least once every week, then you'll know you can have dinner on the table in less than 30 minutes any night at all.

2 cups all-purpose gluten-free flour

1½ teaspoons xanthan gum

1 tablespoon active dry yeast

1 teaspoon sugar

¾ teaspoon kosher salt

¾ cup warm water (about 100°F)

3 tablespoons extra-virgin olive oil (plus an extra tablespoon or two for drizzling)

1. In a medium-size bowl or the bowl of your food processor, place the flour, xanthan gum, yeast, sugar, and salt and stir to combine.

2. To the flour mixture, add the 3 tablespoons of olive oil and the water in a steady stream, either pulsing in a food processor or mixing with a spoon or fork to combine. If you are using a food processor, pulse while streaming in the water, until a ball begins to form. Otherwise, stir constantly while streaming in the water and continue stirring until the mixture begins to come together. If the dough seems super sticky, add some more flour a tablespoon at a time, and stir or pulse to combine. Press the dough into a disk.

3. Place the dough in another medium-size bowl and drizzle it with olive oil. Turn the dough it to coat with oil. This will prevent a crust from forming on the dough while it is rising. Cover the bowl with plastic wrap and place it in a warm, draft-free area to rise until doubled in volume (about 1 hour).

4. After the dough has risen, wrap it in plastic wrap and chill for at least an hour before rolling out.

To make pizza:

Roll out the dough, create a crust by rolling in the edges, brush the dough with olive oil and blind bake it at about 400°F (i.e., bake it plain, before topping it) for 5 to 7 minutes so the crust is crisp. Then, top it with sauce, cheese, and whatever else you have in the fridge, and return it to the hot oven until the cheese is melted, another 5 to 7 minutes.

VARIATIONS

Lay another round of dough on top before baking with the toppings, and voilà: you have stuffed pizza. Roll the dough flat, cut it into 2 x 5-inch rectangles, wrap the dough around a hot dog for a makeshift bun, then bake in a 400°F oven for 7 to 9 minutes. The possibilities are infinite.

Shoestring Savings

Pizza Dough

On a shoestring: $1.08 per crust

If you bought it: $3.10 per crust

Sourdough Starter

MAKES ABOUT 12 OUNCES STARTER (ABOUT 1½ CUPS)

Before you turn the page, all I ask is that you read the recipe and try to get a feel for what it might be like to make your own gluten-free sourdough starter. Even if you decide you're not ready to tackle **Sourdough Bread** (page 96), you may want to try your hand at this sourdough starter, since it takes a few days to get the starter, well, started. I'm willing to bet that once you see how easy it can be to make gluten-free bread, you'll be craving sourdough bread and wishing you had made that starter. Try it. You'll like it!

1 tablespoon active dry yeast
1 cup whole milk, at room temperature
1 cup white rice flour
1 teaspoon sugar

1. In a 1- to 2-quart glass jar (NOT plastic or metal), dissolve the yeast in the milk by stirring with a wooden spoon. Add the rice flour and sugar and mix to combine well. Cover the jar loosely and allow it to sit at room temperature for 2 to 3 hours. Remember that the milk must be at room temperature for it to activate the yeast.

2. The mixture should bubble and appear pock-marked on the surface. It will also likely develop a thin liquid along the top. Stir to incorporate that back into the mixture. Cover the jar again loosely and allow it to sit out on the counter overnight.

3. Repeat the procedure in Step 2 for the next two days, stirring to combine, loosely covering, and then stirring again the next day, all the while leaving the jar of starter out on the counter at room temperature.

4. If you do not plan to use the starter soon, place it, loosely covered, in the refrigerator. You will need to "feed" it before you use it.

How to "Feed" Your Sourdough Starter

1. When you know that you want to use your sourdough starter, you will need to plan at least 4 hours ahead.

2. Remove the starter from the refrigerator, uncover it, and stir it until smooth with a wooden spoon. Remove one cup of the starter and discard it (or donate it to a friend to create another starter).

3. Add ½ cup warm water (about 100°F) and 1 cup white rice flour to the starter. Stir to combine. Allow the starter to sit out at room temperature for at least 4 hours, or overnight, loosely covered. The starter should be bubbling and thick. It is now "fed."

4. Use the amount of starter your recipe calls for, then replenish the starter by feeding it again with ½ cup warm water and 1 cup white rice flour, stirring to combine, cover again loosely, and return it to the refrigerator.

Wonton Wrappers

MAKES 15 TO 20 WONTON WRAPPERS

Did you know how simple it is to make your own wonton wrappers? Not to worry. That's why you and I are having this talk. And you should feel free to pass it off as your idea. Most likely, you and I don't have any friends in common, so we won't show up at the same gluten-free potluck dinner, bearing the very same gluten-free wontons. That would just be embarrassing.

1 cup all-purpose gluten-free flour, plus more for dusting
½ teaspoon xanthan gum
1 extra-large egg and 1 extra-large egg white, beaten together
2 to 4 tablespoons warm water

1. In a medium-size bowl, combine the flour and xanthan gum. Add the eggs and 2 tablespoons water to the flour mixture and beat together to combine.

2. Press the mixture together with wet hands. It should stick together when pressed, and should have a smooth but stiff consistency. Add more water a tablespoon at a time until it reaches the proper consistency.

3. Separate the dough into two disks. Roll out each disk between two sheets of plastic wrap until they're about ⅛ inch thick. Remove the plastic wrap, dust both sides with more flour, and slice into desired shapes with a sharp knife.

4. When you're using the wrappers, moisten the edges with a bit of warm water to help them stick together when cinched closed.

Pâte à Choux
(Light, French-Style Pastry Dough)

Pâte à choux, or choux pastry, a simple but special French pastry, looks (and sounds) just beautiful and is just as versatile. With a small switcharoo of a couple ingredients either way, it can be either savory (**Gougères**, see page 50) or sweet (**Profiteroles**, see page 51). Made the size of dinner rolls, savory or sweet, they are just right served with an omelet for breakfast or brunch. Super-small gougères make delicate cheese puff appetizers. And you only need basic pantry and refrigerator staples, so little to no advance planning is needed to whip up a batch. Beat that with a stick (or a wooden spoon).

1 cup milk (low-fat is fine, nonfat is not)

4 tablespoons unsalted butter

¾ teaspoon kosher salt

⅛ teaspoon freshly ground black pepper (optional)

1 cup all-purpose gluten-free flour

½ teaspoon xanthan gum

4 extra-large eggs

1 extra-large egg, beaten with 1 teaspoon water (for egg wash)

1. Cook the milk, butter, salt, and (optional) pepper in a large saucepan until the butter is melted and the mixture begins to boil.

2. Remove the pan from the heat, add the flour and xanthan gum, and stir vigorously. Return to the heat, and continue to stir vigorously for about 3 minutes, until the mixture pulls away from the sides of the pan and comes together in a ball. A thin film will form on the bottom of the pan.

3. Remove the pan from the heat again, this time for good. Allow the mixture to cool for about 3 to 5 minutes. We're fixing to add the eggs, and we don't want to go scrambling them.

4. Line rimmed baking sheets with parchment paper, and preheat your oven to 425°F.

5. Add the eggs to the dough, one at a time, stirring the mixture vigorously after each addition. With each egg, the mixture will seem somewhat lumpy, leaving you feeling like you wish you had just left well enough alone and not messed with your gorgeous dough. Patience, my friend. Keep beating. You shall be rewarded. The thing will come together quite nicely in the end.

6. Either pipe the dough in mounds through the wide open tip of a pastry bag onto parchment-lined baking sheets, 2 inches apart from one another, or scoop mounds of dough with a 1½-inch ice cream scoop onto those same parchment-lined baking sheets, the same 2 inches apart. If you go the pastry bag route, be sure to flatten the tip of each mound with wet fingertips before baking, or it may burn. Brush each puff lightly with the egg wash.

7. Place baking sheets in the preheated oven and bake 10 minutes at 425°F. Without opening the oven, turn the temperature down to 375°F and finish baking for another 15 to 20 minutes. Five to ten minutes before the end, open the oven quickly and mark a small "x" in the top of each puff with a very sharp knife. This will allow steam to escape and help keep the puffs, well, puffy. Continue baking until golden brown.

8. Allow the puffs to cool at least 5 minutes, 10 if you can stand it. Enjoy with soup, or standing up in the kitchen when no one's looking.

Gougères (Cheese Puffs)

MAKES 12 MEDIUM-SIZE CHEESE PUFFS

To make gougères, add 1 cup grated cheese to the pâte à choux dough after adding the eggs in Step 5 above. You may use any type of grated cheese you like. If authenticity is the name of your game, go with gruyère cheese. I usually use ⅓ cup Parmesan cheese and ⅔ cup gruyère (okay, fine, I use ⅔ cup of whatever other grated cheese I have in my refrigerator), but these must be made with dairy cheese. Sadly, nondairy cheese will just not do here.

Profiteroles (Cream Puffs)

MAKES 12 MEDIUM-SIZE CREAM PUFFS

To make profiteroles, substitute a pinch of salt instead of the ¾ teaspoon and eliminate the egg wash. After baking, split the little beauties in half horizontally, place vanilla ice cream in the center, and drizzle with melted **Chocolate Ganache** (page 236).

SAUCES

These are your basic sauces. They all use a similar set of ingredients, and all stay reasonably well in the refrigerator after being made. The reason is that the acid they contain, in the form of vinegar, keeps them fresh. You make what you need, in the proportions you like, omitting the ingredients you don't care for. You will save tons of change, and you will live a life uncluttered. No longer will your refrigerator door be littered with bottles of dressings and sauces containing varying amounts of aging residue. Imagine the clarity you can achieve. You might very well find yourself writing the next Great American Novel. Think of it as kitchen Feng Shui.

Chinese-Style Hot Sauce

MAKES ABOUT ½ CUP

This hot sauce is an ingredient in **Szechuan Meatballs** (page 151), and it also goes nicely with **Crispy Asian-Style Tofu** (page 138), **Lo Mein** (page 154), and **Beef Potstickers** (page 165).

½ teaspoon ground hot red pepper seeds
4 tablespoons rice vinegar
4 teaspoons tomato paste
4 teaspoons honey or sugar

1. Place all of the ingredients together in a medium-size bowl. Whisk to combine well.

Sweet and Sour Sauce

MAKES ABOUT ¾ CUP

This sauce pairs really well with chicken, but it's also delicious when used to marinate pork loin, or really almost anything fried.

2 tablespoons gluten-free soy sauce (I like La Choy Lite)
1 tablespoon cornstarch
⅓ cup rice vinegar
¼ cup ketchup
4 tablespoons sugar
¾ cup water, at room temperature

1. In a medium-size bowl, whisk together the soy sauce, cornstarch, rice vinegar, ketchup, and sugar until well combined. Add the water and whisk again to combine.

2. Pour the mixture into a medium saucepan and cook over medium-high heat until it is has thickened and is reduced by about half.

Hoisin Sauce

MAKES ABOUT ½ CUP

Like **Chinese-Style Hot Sauce** (page 52), itself an ingredient in **Hoisin Sauce** (page 54), this sauce complements **Szechuan Meatballs** (page 151), **Crispy Asian-Style Tofu** (page 138), **Lo Mein** (page 154), and **Beef Potstickers** (page 165).

4 tablespoons gluten-free soy sauce

2 tablespoons natural peanut butter (or black bean paste, which can be found in most natural food stores and Asian markets)

1 tablespoon honey

2 teaspoons white wine vinegar

⅛ teaspoon garlic powder

2 teaspoons sesame oil

⅛ teaspoon freshly ground black pepper

1½ teaspoons **Chinese-Style Hot Sauce** (optional) (page 52)

1. Place all of the ingredients together in a medium-size bowl. Whisk to combine well.

Barbecue Sauce

MAKES ABOUT 1 CUP

This delicious Barbecue Sauce is a great pairing for any traditional barbecued meat, like roasted chicken parts or ribs, and it also dresses up **Meatlove** (page 162) like a champ.

¾ cup tomato ketchup
2 tablespoons light brown sugar
1 tablespoon white wine vinegar
1 tablespoon Worcestershire sauce
2 teaspoons sweet paprika (optional)
¼ teaspoon cayenne pepper (optional)

1. Place all of the ingredients together in a medium-size bowl. Whisk to combine well.

Blueberry-Cranberry Sauce

MAKES ABOUT 2 CUPS

I make this sauce on a regular basis, and I use it throughout the week to dress lunchtime sliced turkey sandwiches. Sometimes I serve a dollop of blueberry-cranberry sauce atop a steaming bowl of **Chicken and Dumplings** (page 170). Yum! If you live in an area (like mine) that doesn't sell whole cranberries all year round, just buy bags and bags when they are for sale and freeze them. Cranberries make the most beautiful **Berry Scones** (page 82), too.

1 (12-ounce) bag fresh whole cranberries

4–6 ounces frozen (or fresh) blueberries

Scant ⅔ cup sugar

Zest of 1 lemon (optional)

1 cup water

1. Place the cranberries, blueberries, sugar, lemon zest (if using), and water in a medium saucepan. Stir to combine.

2. Bring the mixture to a boil, then reduce the heat and simmer for about 10 minutes, or until the berries are soft and the sauce is as thick as you desire.

3. Allow the sauce to cool. The sauce may be stored in an airtight container in the refrigerator for about 5 days.

Turkey Brine

Everyone has their own way of making a whole turkey, and everyone swears theirs is the best. So rather than joining the chorus, I'll rain on the parade. I think that no matter what you do to turkey, it tastes like turkey. That's why they make things like turducken. Think about it. In any event, when I make turkey, my objectives are threefold: to help the poor bird retain as much of its natural moisture as possible, to reduce the time it has to cook because it cramps my style, and to make "carving" essentially an unnecessary and largely academic exercise. This brine, which makes enough for a 12- to 15-pound turkey, is a success on all three counts. Using it makes a moist turkey, speeds up overall cooking time, and results in meat that basically falls off the bone. (But it still tastes like turkey to me.)

2 gallons (32 cups) water

1½ cups kosher salt

3 tablespoons garlic, minced

1 tablespoon freshly ground black pepper

¼ cup Worcestershire sauce

⅓ cup packed dark brown sugar

New 4- to 5-gallon tub, with tight-fitting lid (a big cooler lined with a plastic bag works well)

1. Boil 6 to 8 cups of water. Once the water boils, dissolve the kosher salt in the hot water.

2. Pour the salt water into the tub and add the remaining 24 to 26 cups of water, the garlic, pepper, Worcestershire sauce, and brown sugar.

3. Add the turkey to the liquid, and press it down so the cavity fills with liquid. Cover the tub and place it in the refrigerator for 24 to 48 hours.

4. To cook the bird, follow the cooking time and temperature as directed on the package for your size turkey.

DIPS AND SNACKS

Cheese Crackers

MAKES 2 DOZEN CRACKERS

These crackers are super simple, seductively elegant, inexpensive to make, and terribly versatile. As described here, they're rounds. But you can make them in any shape you like. Cut the dough into strips, and they're sticks. Roll the strips end over end, and they're sweet little cheese puffs.

1 cup all-purpose gluten-free flour

½ teaspoon xanthan gum

¾ teaspoon kosher salt

1 cup finely grated cheddar cheese

6 tablespoons unsalted butter, diced and chilled

4–6 tablespoons milk (low-fat is fine, nonfat is not), chilled

1. Mix the flour, xanthan gum, and salt in a medium-size bowl until well combined. Add the cheese and stir to combine.

2. Using a handheld pastry blender (or simply two knives, or a food processor, if you prefer), cut the diced butter into the flour mixture until the mixture resembles small peas. Now add the milk to the mixture, tablespoon by tablespoon, first stirring with a large spoon to combine, then squeezing the mixture with clean, wet hands, adding milk and squeezing until the dough comes together into a cohesive ball. Cover the dough in plastic wrap and place it in the refrigerator for at least an hour, up to overnight.

3. Once the dough is chilled, preheat the oven to 325°F. Roll out the dough between two sheets of plastic wrap until it's about the thickness of a nickel (about ⅛ inch thick, for those of you who are wondering what a nickel is). At this point, you could uncover the dough and dust it with more flour. But that extra flour would, of course, cost extra. Instead, the dough will be easy to handle

without an extra dusting of flour if you simply place it, still covered in both sheets of plastic wrap, flat on its back in the refrigerator to chill for another 10 to 15 minutes. In the meanwhile, line baking sheets with parchment paper.

Once the dough has chilled again, use a biscuit cutter to cut rounds and place them evenly spaced, about ½ inch apart on the baking sheets (they don't spread much, if at all, during baking). Place in the preheated oven and bake, rotating halfway through, for 12 to 14 minutes, until pale golden brown (or darker, if you like).

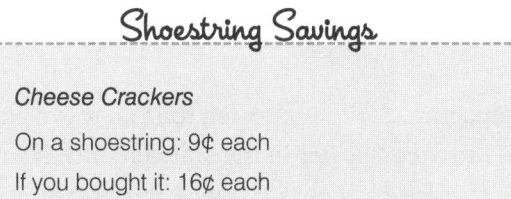

Shoestring Savings

Cheese Crackers

On a shoestring: 9¢ each

If you bought it: 16¢ each

Spinach Dip

MAKES 6 TO 8 SERVINGS

You can serve this flavorful, creamy spinach dip in a hollowed-out "bread bowl," but there's no way I'd waste a loaf of gluten-free bread by using it as a serving bowl. That would be madness. I just serve it with some chips or some sliced raw vegetables.

2 (10-ounce) packages frozen chopped spinach, thawed
½ cup (4 ounces) cream cheese (low-fat is fine, nonfat is not)
½ cup (4 ounces) mayonnaise (low-fat is fine, nonfat is not)
¼ cup freshly grated Parmesan cheese
½ cup grated mozzarella cheese
Juice of 1 large lemon
3 garlic cloves, minced
1 teaspoon dried parsley flakes
Kosher salt and freshly ground black pepper, to taste

1. Place the spinach in a kitchen towel, roll the towel closed, and twist the towel to wring out the excess water in the spinach until it wrings dry.

2. In the bowl of a food processor, place the cream cheese, mayonnaise, Parmesan and mozzarella cheeses, lemon juice, garlic, parsley, salt, and pepper and process until smooth. Add the spinach to the mixture and fold it in until the spinach is evenly distributed throughout the dip. Transfer the mixture to a serving bowl and serve chilled or at room temperature.

Traditional Hummus

MAKES ABOUT 2 CUPS

These days, there are many brands of prepared hummus that are reliably gluten-free and taste quite good. In my local market, though, they cost nearly four times as much as making hummus yourself. And when you make it yourself, you can make **Roasted Red Pepper Hummus** (page 62), or even use **Scratch Black Beans** (page 37) instead of garbanzo beans for **Black Bean Hummus** (page 63). And it lasts for at least a week in the refrigerator. The only new ingredient you may have to begin stocking is tahini (sesame paste), which is usually available in conventional supermarkets, on the shelf near the nut butters, but a little of it goes a long way.

2 (15-ounce) cans garbanzo beans, drained (not rinsed)
1½ teaspoons kosher salt
4 cloves of garlic, minced
⅓ cup tahini (sesame paste)
Juice of 2 lemons
¼ teaspoon lemon zest (optional)
2–4 tablespoons extra-virgin olive oil

1. In the bowl of a standard-size food processor fitted with the steel blade, place the garbanzo beans, salt, garlic, tahini, lemon juice, and (optional) lemon zest. Process until smooth. Add a tablespoon or two of water if necessary to smooth out the texture.

2. With the food processor switched on, drizzle in 2 tablespoons olive oil. Add up to 2 more tablespoons, to taste.

Roasted Red Pepper Hummus

MAKES ABOUT 2 CUPS

2 (15-ounce) cans garbanzo beans, drained (not rinsed)

1½ teaspoons kosher salt

4 cloves of garlic, minced

⅓ cup tahini (sesame paste)

Juice of 2 lemons

2 large **Roasted Red Peppers** (page 38), chopped and drained of oil, if necessary

2–4 tablespoons extra-virgin olive oil

1. In the bowl of a standard-size food processor fitted with the steel blade, add the garbanzo beans, salt, garlic, tahini, lemon juice, and red peppers. Process until smooth. Add a tablespoon or two of water if necessary to smooth out the texture.

2. With the food processor switched on, drizzle in 2 tablespoons olive oil. Add up to 2 more tablespoons, to taste.

Black Bean Hummus

MAKES ABOUT 2 CUPS

3½ cups **Scratch Black Beans** (page 37) or 2 (15-ounce) cans black beans, drained but
   not rinsed
1½ teaspoons kosher salt
4 cloves of garlic, minced
⅓ cup tahini (sesame paste)
Juice of 2 lemons
¼ teaspoon lemon zest (optional)
2–4 tablespoons extra-virgin olive oil

1. In the bowl of a standard-size food processor fitted with the steel blade,
add the black beans, salt, garlic, tahini, lemon juice, and (optional) lemon zest.
Process until smooth. Add a tablespoon or two of water if necessary to smooth
out the texture.

2. With the food processor switched on, drizzle in 2 tablespoons olive oil.
Add up to 2 more tablespoons, to taste.

Four

Breakfast and Brunch, Just as You Remember Them

Tortilla Española

SERVES 6 TO 8 PEOPLE FOR BRUNCH OR LIGHT DINNER,
OR MANY MORE AS AN APPETIZER

A Spanish tortilla is nothing like the bread-like **Flour Tortillas** in the chapter on Breads (see page 120). It's more like an omelette with onions and potatoes and is often served at room temperature as a light dinner, or for brunch. Although I usually dislike using a nonstick pan, as I feel that it's never truly clean even after washing it thoroughly and prefer instead the enameled cast iron of a Dutch oven, a nonstick skillet is essential to making a Tortilla Española. This way you can cook down the sliced potatoes slowly without having them stick to the pan and flip the tortilla easily. I have a shallow 10-inch nonstick skillet that I bought largely to be able to make this dish properly. It's also great for shallow frying anything dredged in eggs, like breaded chicken cutlets, and I find it essential for making **Arepas** (page 136). Never say never.

4 tablespoons olive or vegetable oil

5 to 6 medium-size red-skin or yellow-skin potatoes, peeled and sliced ⅛ inch thick

1 large or 2 medium yellow onions, chopped

1 tablespoon kosher salt

Freshly ground black pepper, to taste

10 extra-large eggs

1. In a 10-inch or 12-inch nonstick skillet, heat the oil over medium-high heat, add onions, and cook for about 6 minutes, until mostly translucent. (If you don't have such a large nonstick skillet, split the recipe in half and use a smaller pan for each half, working in shifts; no big deal.) Then add the potatoes, salt, and pepper, then cover and cook, stirring occasionally, for about 20 minutes, until the potatoes are wilted and soft.

2. While the potatoes are cooking away, beat the eggs in a separate bowl (one with a lip, if you have it), adding just a tiny amount of salt and pepper (the potatoes are already seasoned, remember). When the potatoes are ready, pour the eggs over the top of the potatoes and press them down so they are immersed in the egg and the top of the mixture is relatively even. Cook over very low heat, covered, about 15 minutes, until the egg is nearly set. Then remove from the heat and let stand about 5 to 10 minutes covered (until the top is completely set).

3. It's time to flip the tortilla over, so we can brown the underside. It's much easier than it sounds. First, gently shake the skillet to make sure that the tortilla is not stuck to the bottom of the pan. If it does seem a bit stuck, run a heatproof spatula along the edge of the tortilla to free it. Now place a large plate firmly on top of the skillet and, stepping lively, invert the plate and skillet together. Remove the skillet from the top. Now simply slide the tortilla from the plate back into the skillet, shimmying the plate as you go.

4. All that's left to do is cover and cook again over very low heat for about 5 minutes. Slide off the skillet and onto a plate and serve either warm or at room temperature. There are a few traditional Spanish ways to serve it: for tapas, cut it into squares with toothpicks inserted into each square or separate off a rectangle of the tortilla and serve it on a roll.

Ricotta Pancakes

MAKES 4 SERVINGS

This is the only traditional pancake that I consider worth my slaving over a hot stove, flipping the second batch while everyone else enjoys the first one. Under all other circumstances, I make **Banana Pancake Muffins** (page 86). Ricotta Pancakes are the one exception, and when you try them, you'll understand why!

⅔ cup all-purpose gluten-free flour

⅓ teaspoon xanthan gum

⅓ cup sugar

1 teaspoon baking powder

2 extra-large eggs, beaten

1 cup ricotta cheese

Finely grated zest of 1 lemon

½ cup milk (low-fat is fine, nonfat is not)

2–3 tablespoons vegetable oil

1. In a large bowl, place the flour, xanthan gum, sugar, and baking powder, and whisk to combine. Add the eggs, ricotta cheese, lemon zest, and milk, beating well after each addition.

2. Coat the bottom of a large nonstick skillet with vegetable oil and use about ¼ cup batter for each pancake. Cook the first side over medium heat for about 4 minutes, or until bubbles form on top. Flatten the pancakes with a spatula as they cook, because they will remain raw inside if they are too thick. Flip to brown the other side and serve immediately.

Oven Hash Brown Quiche

MAKES 4 TO 6 SERVINGS

I often make oven hash browns. I just peel and grate potatoes, wring them dry, then toss them with kosher salt, pepper, and canola oil and bake them in a rimmed baking sheet in one layer in a 400°F oven for 15 to 20 minutes. Then I cut the hash browns into squares with kitchen shears and serve topped with scrambled eggs. It's super tasty, easy, inexpensive, and even looks elegant. This quiche starts with the same principle, but uses the oven hash browns as a crust for a quiche. Crispy on the underside and creamy toward the middle, it makes for lovely brunch.

4 medium potatoes (yellow-skin or red-skin potatoes), peeled and grated

Kosher salt and freshly ground black pepper, to taste

3–4 tablespoons vegetable oil

8 ounces frozen broccoli

8 extra-large eggs

12 ounces evaporated milk (low-fat is fine, nonfat is not; for a nondairy substitute, try simmering nondairy milk in a small pot until reduced by half)

4 ounces grated cheddar or mozzarella cheese

4 ounces grated Parmesan cheese

1. Preheat your oven to 375°F. Grease a 9-inch glass pie plate with unsalted butter and set it aside.

2. Place the grated potatoes in a kitchen towel, wring to squeeze out as much water from the potatoes as possible, and then place them in a large bowl. Toss the potatoes with salt and pepper to taste and the vegetable oil. Press the potatoes evenly into the bottom and sides of the prepared pie plate. Place the pie plate into the center of the preheated oven and bake for 10 to 15 minutes, or until the potatoes are just beginning the brown on top and around the bottom. You're using a glass pie plate so you can sneak a look at the crust as it browns.

3. While the hash brown crust is browning, defrost and drain the broccoli, then chop it into bite-size pieces. In a large bowl, whisk together the eggs, milk, and salt and pepper to taste. Stir in the grated cheese and broccoli.

4. Remove the hash brown crust from the oven and pour the egg mixture into the center of the pie plate. Place the quiche in the center of the oven and bake for about 35 to 45 minutes, or until the eggs are set and golden around the edges, and you can see by looking through the bottom of the pie plate that the crust has browned nicely.

5. Slice into wedges and serve immediately.

Apple-Cinnamon Toaster Pastries

MAKES 6 TOASTER PASTRIES

You could use the **Sweet Pastry Crust** (page 39) recipe in Chapter 3 instead of the pastry recipe I use here and still be pleased with the results. I just tweaked the pastry here a bit to make it more robust. But if you either really love the Sweet Pastry Crust recipe, or, better yet, happen to have some on hand leftover from another recipe, by all means make good use of it. Waste not, want not.

PASTRY

1¼ cups all-purpose gluten-free flour

Scant ¾ teaspoon xanthan gum

½ teaspoon kosher salt

¼ teaspoon baking powder

⅓ cup confectioner's sugar

1 stick (8 tablespoons) unsalted butter, diced and chilled

½ cup ice-cold milk (low-fat is fine, nonfat is not)

FILLING

2 empire apples, peeled, cored, and cut into a small dice

½ teaspoon pure vanilla extract

⅛ teaspoon kosher salt

½ teaspoon ground cinnamon

4 tablespoons packed brown sugar

1 teaspoon cornstarch

1. Make the pastry dough first, since it must chill before completing the recipe. To make the pastry, in a large bowl, mix the flour, xanthan gum, salt, baking powder, and confectioner's sugar until the ingredients are all well combined.

2. Add the diced butter to the bowl of dry ingredients. If you have a pastry blender, cut in the butter by holding on to the handle and pressing the tines of the blender into the mixture over and over again until the mixture resembles small peas of butter wrapped in the flour mixture. If you are using two knives,

just cross them and cut repeatedly into the mixture until the mixture arrives at small peas of butter wrapped in the flour mixture.

3. Add the ice-cold milk to the mixture and stir to combine. Place plastic sandwich bags on your hands (the old-school, fold-over kind, not the zipper bags) and squeeze the mixture together tightly in your fists. If the mixture does not hold together, take off the plastic bags, add another tablespoon of ice-cold milk, and squeeze again until you are able to form a respectable ball with your hands. You want to try to handle the dough as little as possible, within reason, so you don't melt the butter. Once you have created a ball, wrap it in plastic wrap and place it in the refrigerator. Chill for at least 30 minutes, or as long as overnight.

4. While the pastry is chilling, make the filling. In a medium saucepan, place the apples, vanilla, salt, and cinnamon, plus 2 tablespoons of water, and stir to combine. Cook, over medium-high heat, for about 10 minutes, stirring frequently, until the apples are very soft. Once the apple mixture is cooked, remove the saucepan from the heat and stir in the brown sugar and cornstarch. Stir until the sugar and cornstarch are dissolved, with no lumps of either.

5. Preheat your oven to 400°F. Line baking sheets with parchment paper and set aside.

6. Once the pastry dough has chilled, remove it from the refrigerator and place it between two large sheets of plastic wrap. Roll the dough between the plastic wrap until it is a rectangle, about ⅛ inch thick (no thinner). Carefully remove and replace one piece of plastic wrap, invert the dough, and carefully remove the other sheet of plastic wrap. With a very sharp knife, delicately cut the large rectangle of dough into twelve same-size rectangles. Divide the filling evenly among six of the pastry rectangles, spreading out the filling but leaving a border of about ½ inch from the edges. Place the remaining six pastry rectangles atop the six with filling and, using the tines of a fork, press down the edges of the pastry to seal them.

7. Remove the pastries from the underlying plastic wrap and place each carefully on the lined baking sheets, about 1 inch apart. Bake for 10 to 12 minutes, or until the pastries are lightly golden brown. Serve immediately.

Homemade Crunchy Granola

MAKES ABOUT 5 CUPS

Even conventional granola is one of those foods that can cost you a king's ran-som, but it seems that no one knows why that is. And don't get me started on the cost of gluten-free granola. Take heart, though, dear friends: you can create your own homemade, gluten-free granola, modified to your particular tastes, whichever way they run, and have it all done before you can say "Bob's your un-cle." The almonds and the oats are somewhat compulsory, or it's not really gra-nola, and you'll certainly need some honey and some oil. But the dried fruit you choose is your business. Just be sure add it to the granola toward the end of baking and finish the granola off at a lower oven temperature to prevent the fruit from hardening.

4 tablespoons canola oil

8 tablespoons honey

½ teaspoon kosher salt

3 cups old-fashioned certified gluten-free rolled oats (be careful: not all oats are gluten-free)

1 cup sliced almonds

½ cup dried cranberries (preferably unsweetened)

½ cup raisins

1. Preheat your oven to 350°F. Line a rimmed baking sheet with parchment paper and set it aside.

2. In a small saucepan over low heat, heat the oil, honey, and salt, stirring oc-casionally, until the honey has melted and the mixture is warmed throughout (3 to 5 minutes).

3. While the honey and oil are warming, in a separate large bowl, add the oats and almonds, and stir until well combined. When the honey mixture is ready, pour it over the oat mixture and stir with a wet spatula (to prevent the honey from clumping) until the honey mixture has coated the oat mixture com-pletely. Scrape the mixture onto the prepared baking sheet and spread it out in a single, even layer.

4. Place the baking sheet in the center of the preheated oven and bake for approximately 15 minutes or until golden brown. To ensure even baking, rotate the baking sheet once during baking, and stir the granola once along the way as well. Remove the baking sheet from the oven and reduce the heat to 300°F. Allow the granola to cool for about 10 minutes on the baking sheet and then return it to the large bowl, add the cranberries and raisins, and stir until they are evenly distributed throughout the granola. Spread the granola out in a single layer on the baking sheet.

5. Return the baking sheet to the oven and bake for another 5 to 10 minutes, until the granola is a pale golden brown. Cool the granola completely on the baking sheet. It can be stored in an airtight container at room temperature for at least two weeks.

Plain Bagels

MAKES 10 REGULAR-SIZE (NOT JUMBO) BAGELS

My son came home one day and announced, nice as you please, that tomorrow he would be needing a green bagel for a St. Patrick's Day celebration in school— where of course, everyone else would be eating a gluten-filled green bagel. The moral of the story is this: you never know when such an announcement might be made in your house. (And if it is, a few drops of plain, water-based Mc-Cormick's green food-coloring in the warm water called for in the recipe below is all you need). So you've got to be prepared. It is with these sorts of adventures in mind that I present the following never-fail basic bagel recipe; see chapter 5 for cinnamon raisin and seeded options.

Making bagels is deceptively simple, but it does tend to require some extra cleanup. You have to dredge the dough in some extra flour to make it easier to handle, and then you have to boil the bagels before you bake them. When you boil them, be sure to do it in a large pot of water since, like dumplings, they swell when they're boiling.

4 cups all-purpose gluten-free flour (plus extra for dusting)

3 teaspoons xanthan gum

1 tablespoon kosher salt

1 tablespoon active dry yeast

6 tablespoons honey

2–3 cups warm water (about 100°F)

2 tablespoons sugar

1 extra-large egg, beaten with 1 tablespoon water (for egg wash)

1. In a large bowl, place the flour, xanthan gum, salt, and yeast and whisk to combine. To the dry ingredients, add the honey and mix to distribute. It will sort of clump a bit, and that's fine.

2. In a slow but steady stream, add 2 cups of the water, mixing with a spoon as you pour. Mix until the dough begins to come together. If it is not coming to-gether, add more water a bit at a time, mixing as you go, until it comes together.

The dough should be thick and sticky, but not impossible to handle. Divide the dough into ten heaped portions, sprinkling each portion with a light dusting of flour and rolling it gently between the palms of your hands into a disk about 1¼ inches thick. With a well-floured index finger, create a small hole in the center of each disk. Move your finger in a gentle circular motion to widen the hole. Turn the disk over and repeat the procedure on the other side.

3. Place the mounds of dough about 1 inch apart on a rimmed baking sheet lined with parchment paper and allow them to rise in a warm, moist place for 30 to 45 minutes until the dough has risen to about one and a half times its original size. In cool, dry weather, the dough may take longer to rise; in warm, moist weather, it may take less time to rise.

4. While the bagels are rising, boil a pot or pan full of water, at least 6 inches deep. Dissolve the sugar in the boiling water. After the bagels have risen, gently place the mounds of dough into the boiling water, two at a time, for 3 minutes total. Gently turn over the bagels halfway through boiling.

5. As they finish boiling, place each bagel back on the parchment paper–lined baking sheets, about 1 inch apart. With a pastry brush, brush each bagel generously with the egg wash.

6. At this point, the bagels can be frozen on the baking sheets until solid, then placed in freezer-safe resealable plastic bags to be baked another time. They should be thawed for at least 2 hours at room temperature before baking (or you can stick them in the "defrost" mode in your microwave for a bit for a quick defrost, but you'll be a little sad if you do that since they won't turn out quite as good).

7. Once you are ready to bake them, preheat the oven to 375°F. Place the bagels about 1 inch apart on the parchment paper–lined baking sheets in the preheated oven and bake them for about 25 minutes, or until golden brown.

8. Allow the bagels to cool at least 15 to 20 minutes before slicing them open, even though it's hard and you've been waiting oh-so-long.

Shoestring Savings

Plain Bagels

On a shoestring: 44¢ per bagel

If you bought it: $1.28 per bagel (frozen)

Cinnamon Rolls

MAKES 12 CINNAMON ROLLS

Truth? These require a bit of advance planning. They have to be made the night before, refrigerated overnight, and baked first thing in the morning. And then you have to eat them right away, which is seemingly much less of a problem than the advance planning part. But if you have guests you want to impress, or you're suddenly feeling all warm and fuzzy toward your family one night, treat them to cinnamon rolls the next day. Just be sure to get lots of mileage out of the extra work you put in.

DOUGH

6 tablespoons unsalted butter, melted and cooled to room temperature

¼ cup sugar

2 extra-large eggs, plus 3 extra-large egg yolks, at room temperature

1½ cups milk at room temperature (low-fat is fine, nonfat is not), plus 1 tablespoon white wine vinegar (or 1½ cup buttermilk at room temperature), shaken to combine well

3 cups all-purpose gluten-free flour

2 teaspoons xanthan gum

1 teaspoon kosher salt

1 tablespoon active dry yeast

FILLING

¾ cup light brown sugar, packed

2 tablespoons unsalted butter, melted and cooled

2 teaspoons ground cinnamon

⅛ teaspoon kosher salt

1. In a large bowl, cream the butter and sugar until light and fluffy. Add the eggs and egg yolks, one at a time, and the milk and vinegar mixture, beating well after each addition until the mixture is smooth. To the wet ingredients, add 2 cups of the flour and the xanthan gum, salt, and yeast, beating well after each addition. Beat the mixture until it becomes thicker and a bit more elastic to ac-

tivate the xanthan gum. Add the remaining cup of flour and mix until the dough comes together. The dough will be sticky, but you should be able to handle it with some maneuvering. If it seems super sticky, add more flour a tablespoon at a time and stir to combine.

2. Grease a 9 x 13-inch baking dish with unsalted butter and set it aside. To make the filling, in a medium bowl, place the sugar, butter, cinnamon, and salt and mix with a fork until a paste forms. Set the bowl aside.

3. Place the dough between two sheets of plastic wrap. Roll the dough between the two sheets of plastic wrap into a square that is approximately 12 x 12 inches. Remove and replace one sheet of plastic wrap, and then flip over the dough and remove the other sheet of plastic wrap. Spread the filling mixture onto the exposed side of the dough, gently so as to avoid tearing the dough and leaving about a 1-inch border free of filling all around the dough. Moisten the bare 1-inch border with wet fingers. Beginning with one side of the dough, roll the dough (only) into a cylinder as tightly as possible, pinch the seam to seal it well, and place it on the flat surface seam-side down. Slice the cylinder into 12 cross-sections, each about 1 inch thick. Arrange the cinnamon rolls about 1 inch apart in the prepared baking dish.

4. Cover the baking dish tightly with plastic wrap and place it in a warm, draft-free area to rise until the rolls have doubled in volume (about 1 hour). Once the rolls have risen, place the baking dish, still covered in plastic wrap, in the refrigerator overnight.

5. In the morning, remove the rolls from the refrigerator and preheat your oven to 350°F. Remove the plastic wrap from the baking dish and place it in the center of the preheated oven and bake for about 30 minutes, or until golden brown. Serve immediately.

Banana-Blueberry Muffins

MAKES 12 MUFFINS

Moist and flavorful, but not overly sweet, these muffins are a big hit in my house. The bright blueberries also make for a beautiful presentation. They are made with sour cream, which is often on sale for a steal and lends a tang and a certain substance to this tempting muffin.

1 stick (8 tablespoons) unsalted butter, at room temperature

⅔ cup sugar

1 teaspoon pure vanilla extract

1 extra-large egg, at room temperature

½ cup sour cream (low-fat is fine, nonfat is not)

2 medium-size ripe bananas, 1 mashed and 1 diced

1½ cups all-purpose gluten free flour

¾ teaspoon xanthan gum

1½ teaspoons baking powder

¼ teaspoon baking soda

¼ teaspoon kosher salt

¾ cup frozen blueberries

1. Preheat the oven to 350°F. Grease or line a standard 12-cup muffin tin with unsalted butter and set it aside.

2. In a large bowl, cream the butter and the sugar until light and fluffy. Add the vanilla and the egg and mix until well combined. Next, add in the sour cream, and then the mashed banana, and mix again until well blended. Add the flour, xanthan gum, baking powder, baking soda, and salt to the wet ingredients, reserving a few tablespoons of flour in a separate small bowl. Beat the batter well until it becomes thicker and a bit more elastic, which means that the xanthan gum has been activated.

3. Carefully fold the diced bananas into the batter. Toss the blueberries in the reserved flour, and carefully fold them into the batter as well. Divide the batter evenly among the twelve prepared muffin cups.

4. Place the muffin tin into the center of the preheated oven and bake at 350°F for 20 to 25 minutes, or until the muffins are brown around the edges and a toothpick inserted into the center of the middle muffin comes out with a few moist crumbs attached.

Shoestring Savings

Banana-Blueberry Muffins

On a shoestring: 33¢ per muffin

If you bought it: $2.00 per muffin

Old-Fashioned Gluten-Free Corn Bread

MAKES 8 SERVINGS

Corn bread is a big favorite in my house. Cornmeal is one of my hands-down favorite gluten-free ingredients: since it's naturally gluten-free, even though I mail order it from a source that I am sure processes it free of cross-contamination, it remains inexpensive. And because this recipe uses only cornmeal, rather than a mix of cornmeal and all-purpose gluten-free flour, the cost stays way down. So long as you keep cornmeal in your well-stocked pantry, you'll never be more than about an hour away from corn bread. It's great for **Apple-Leek-Sausage Corn Bread Stuffing** (page 152), and we also love it with a dollop of preserves for breakfast.

½ stick (4 tablespoons) unsalted butter, melted and cooled

2 extra-large eggs, at room temperature

4 tablespoons honey

1¾ cups sour cream

2 cups coarse yellow cornmeal

1 teaspoon kosher salt

1 teaspoon baking soda

2 teaspoons baking powder

1. Preheat the oven to 400°F. Grease an 8-inch square baking dish with unsalted butter and set it aside.

2. In a large bowl, place the butter, eggs, and honey and beat until well combined. Add the sour cream and mix to combine thoroughly. Add the cornmeal, salt, baking soda, and baking powder, blending well after each addition.

3. Pour the mixture into the prepared baking dish, place it in the center of the preheated oven, and bake for 25 to 30 minutes, until the corn bread is firm and a toothpick inserted into the center comes out clean.

Shoestring Savings

Old-Fashioned Gluten-free Cornbread

On a shoestring: $3.65 for 8 servings

If you bought it: $7.00 for 8 servings (frozen)

Bread Pudding

MAKES 4 TO 6 SERVINGS

Bread pudding is a creature of tough economic times, when nothing went to waste. And in this noble spirit of thrift, I would never use fresh gluten-free bread to make bread pudding. Not only does fresh bread make inferior bread pudding (just as it makes inferior French toast), but fresh gluten-free bread should be enjoyed responsibly and respectfully. Bread pudding is where stale gluten-free bread is respectfully laid to rest.

¾ cup granulated sugar

5 extra-large eggs, beaten

2 cups milk (low-fat is fine, nonfat is not)

2 teaspoons pure vanilla extract

3 cups cubed, stale gluten-free bread

¾ cup packed light brown sugar

¼ cup unsalted butter, at room temperature

1 cup chopped pecans (optional)

1. Preheat your oven to 350°F. Grease a 9 x 13-inch baking dish with unsalted butter and set it aside.

2. In a large bowl, place the sugar, eggs, milk, and vanilla and whisk to combine. Place the cubes of bread in the bowl and allow to sit for a few minutes so the bread can soak up the milk mixture.

3. In another small bowl, combine the brown sugar, butter, and (optional) pecans.

4. Pour bread mixture evenly into the prepared baking dish. Scatter the brown sugar mixture over the top of the bread mixture. Bake for about 40 minutes, or until the egg is set.

Berry Scones

MAKES 8 SCONES

As with any pastry, the trick here is to keep the diced butter cold, which makes for light scones, the only sort of scones to have. I like to cut these into triangles, but rounds are lovely, too. My favorite is cranberry scones. The rich red color of the cranberries against the pale golden scones makes me wish they could just sit out on my counter all day long wrapped loosely in a kitchen towel. But once you and your family experience the moist flakiness of these lightly sweet scones, you'll know why they never seem to brighten your kitchen counter for very long.

2 cups all-purpose gluten-free flour

1 teaspoon xanthan gum

1 tablespoon baking powder

½ teaspoon kosher salt

2 tablespoons sugar

1 cup frozen berries (I love cranberries or blueberries here)

5 tablespoons unsalted butter, diced and chilled

1 cup milk (low-fat is fine, nonfat is not)

1. Preheat your oven to 400°F. Line baking sheets with parchment paper and set them aside.

2. Combine the flour, xanthan gum, baking powder, salt, and sugar in a large bowl. Transfer a few tablespoons of this dry ingredient mixture to a small bowl and add the frozen berries. Toss to coat the berries and set aside the small bowl.

3. To the large bowl with the dry ingredients, add the diced butter. Cut it in until the butter resembles pea-size chunks covered in flour. You can either use a pastry cutter or two knives and pretend like you're cutting steak with them over and over.

4. Add the milk to the dry ingredient/butter mixture and stir to combine. The dough will come together. Once the dough has come together, add the berries to the dough and gently fold them in until they are evenly distributed throughout. Handling it as little as possible to keep the butter from melting in

your hands, turn the dough out onto a lightly floured surface and pat it into a rectangle about ½ inch thick.

5. Cut the dough into 8 triangles. Transfer the triangles to baking sheets lined with parchment paper, a couple of inches apart. Brush with a bit of milk and sprinkle with a tiny bit of sugar, if you like.

6. Bake for 15 to 20 minutes, until the scones are puffed up and slightly brown around the edges. Serve immediately.

Shoestring Savings

Berry Scones

On a shoestring: 42¢ per scone

If you bought it: $1.75 per scone (frozen)

Coffee Cake

MAKES 6 TO 8 SERVINGS

Coffee cake is usually served for breakfast or brunch. It is best described as a cake-like bread, usually made with nuts or fruit, and not as sweet as more traditional cakes. This coffee cake, served with coffee or tea, is the perfect "little something" for when you're feeling peckish.

1 stick (8 tablespoons) unsalted butter, at room temperature
¾ cup sugar
3 extra-large eggs, beaten
1 teaspoon pure vanilla extract
1½ cups all-purpose gluten-free flour
¾ teaspoon xanthan gum
1 teaspoon baking powder
1 teaspoon baking soda
½ teaspoon kosher salt
1 teaspoon ground cinnamon
1 cup sour cream (low-fat is fine, nonfat is not)
1 cup raisins (soaked in warm water for 10 minutes and then drained)
1 recipe **Crumble Topping** (page 237), chilled in the refrigerator for at least 30 minutes

1. Preheat your oven to 350°F. Grease a 9-inch round springform pan with unsalted butter and set it aside.

2. In a large bowl, beat the butter and sugar until light and fluffy. Add the egg and vanilla, blending well after each addition. Add the flour, xanthan gum, baking powder, baking soda, salt, and cinnamon, reserving a few tablespoons of flour in a small bowl and beating well after each addition. Next, add the sour cream and stir to combine. After adding the final ingredient, beat until the mixture becomes thicker and a bit more elastic. To the small bowl with the reserved flour, add the drained raisins, and toss to coat. Fold the raisins with the reserved flour into the batter until they are evenly distributed throughout.

3. Pour the cake batter into the prepared pan and spread evenly. Remove the topping from the refrigerator and crumble it with your fingers evenly over the batter.

4. Place the pan in the center of the preheated oven and bake for approximately 45 minutes or until a toothpick inserted into the center of the cake comes out with a few moist crumbs attached. Check the cake after 35 minutes or so. If the topping is browning too quickly, tent the cake loosely with foil and continue baking until done.

Banana Pancake Muffins

MAKES 12 PANCAKE MUFFINS

These light and fluffy little pancake muffins are baked in the oven until they're a pale golden brown. You can serve them nearly straight from the oven, or even refrigerate and reheat them the next day. They don't eat like traditional muffins, since the batter is no different than pancakes cooked on a griddle or in a pan. They taste like, well, banana pancakes, but you can hold them in your hand, and everyone can eat together since they're all ready at the same time. This recipe can also be used to make traditional pancakes of any size and shape.

2 cups all-purpose gluten-free flour

2 teaspoons xanthan gum

½ teaspoon baking soda

1 teaspoon baking powder

1 teaspoon kosher salt

2 tablespoons sugar

1 extra-large egg, lightly beaten

1½ cups milk (low-fat is fine, nonfat is not)

1½ teaspoons white wine vinegar

2 tablespoons unsalted butter, melted and cooled

2 ripe bananas, diced

1. Preheat your oven to 375°F. Grease a standard 12-cup muffin tin with unsalted butter and set it aside.

2. Place the flour, xanthan gum, baking soda, baking powder, salt, and sugar in a large bowl and mix to combine. Add the egg, milk, vinegar, and butter, mixing after each addition. Beat the batter well until it becomes thicker and a bit more elastic. Add the diced bananas to the batter and fold gently until they are evenly distributed throughout.

3. Ladle the pancake batter into the muffin tin and bake for about 20 minutes, or just until the muffins are not wet in the middle. If you have extra batter,

bake the rest in another prepared muffin tin. If not every well is filled with batter, fill the empty wells with water so the baking is even.

4. Cool for 5 minutes in the muffin tin, then serve when still warm.

Shoestring Savings

Banana Pancake Muffins

On a shoestring: $2.70 for 12 muffins

If you bought a mix (and still made it yourself):
    $7.67 for 12 muffins

Five

The Greatest Thing Since . . . Bread, Glorious Bread

Arise, Fair Gluten-Free Bread

Baking gluten-free yeast bread can seem a somewhat mysteriously tall task, but it needn't be, really. It's heaps easier once you know a few facts about gluten-free flours and how they behave and after you read on and learn a few techniques that have served me well. Because let's face it, if your yeast bread is a flop, nobody's saving any money.

Gluten-free flours are heavier than conventional flours, and they are also water-loving. All that means is that gluten-free yeast breads rise best in a *warm, humid environment*. I know many people are accustomed to rising bread in a 200°F oven, which creates a warm environment, but also an inhospitably dry one. If it has ever worked for you, it was a bit of a fluke. You're counting on your bread to rise to the occasion, so you want a fail-safe method.

You can create the proper environment in any tightly enclosed space, like a microwave oven, with a very wet kitchen towel that has been heated until *hot* (I heat mine on high for a full minute). My preferred enclosed space is a microwave oven, but in a pinch I have also used a large Rubbermaid container with a tight-sealing lid, and it works a treat, too. You will still need a heated wet towel, though. If you don't have a microwave, you could try pouring boiling hot water on the kitchen towel, and then going from there.

So you've prepared your dough, and it's ready to rise. Cover the dough loosely in plastic wrap and heat the towel. Once the towel is wet and steaming hot, quickly place the dough, covered in plastic wrap and topped with the steaming hot towel, inside the container of your choice (for me, my microwave), and seal that container in a hurry. Next, allow the dough to rise for about 25 minutes in that controlled environment (absolutely NO peeking), then check. If the dough has not risen enough (or at all), that's totally normal. Don't worry. Just remove the dough from the container, rewet and rewarm the towel, and place the dough back in the container with the hot towel. Check again after another 15 to 20 minutes, give or take. Every once in a while, I have to do a third go-round of about 15 minutes, but it's rare. You should be good to go.

A few other words to the wise: be sure that any liquid you are using as an ingredient in the dough is no more than 100°F, or you risk killing the yeast, and be sure the salt is mixed in with the flour before the yeast is added or it, too, could potentially kill the yeast. Both of these events are relatively rarely the problem. And as long as your yeast is not past its "use by" date, there really is no need to proof it. It's alive. Trust me. Tempting as it is to blame the yeast for not performing, it's generally fine unless it's past its date.

Please remember that gluten-free bread dough is stickier and much more fragile than its conventional counterparts, so don't skimp on water in an effort to create dough that can be rolled, for example, without benefit of plastic wrap. Similarly, don't be afraid to add a bit more flour if you feel you have added too much water and the dough is too sticky. It's not *that* sensitive.

When you're making a loaf of bread that doesn't require any shaping (just scraping into a pan), sticky dough is no biggie. But when you're making something like **French Bread** (see page 91), you need to be able to roll it out between two sheets of plastic wrap, so you may have to add more gluten-free flour by the teaspoonful to achieve the right consistency. Once you have rolled the dough out into a rectangle, sprinkle the outside of the dough with just enough extra gluten-free flour to make handling it possible. It's not going to torpedo the recipe. And please remember the significance of the environment in your kitchen. Some days will be more humid and rising will come easier and perhaps take less time; some days the opposite will be true and you'll need to add more water. Whenever you're working with yeast, the amount of water the recipe calls for is approximate; think of it like an average. Trust your instincts. If it seems way too wet to handle, add some flour. If it seems way too dry and crumbly, add some water. And *always* use plastic wrap when rolling out gluten-free dough.

French Bread

MAKES TWO 12-INCH LOAVES

With just a few ingredients, this recipe can be mastered in no time. Slice a loaf of French bread into rounds, butter and rub it with some raw garlic, then place it on a baking sheet and bake it in a 400°F oven for 7 to 10 minutes, and you've got garlic bread. Split a loaf in the middle, length-wise, layer in some fillings, and you have a hoagie (or a hero or a grinder or a sub, whatever you call it) that rivals any conventional gluten-containing sandwich you can imagine.

3 cups all-purpose gluten-free flour, plus more for dusting

2¼ teaspoons xanthan gum

1 tablespoon sugar

2 teaspoons kosher salt

1 tablespoon active dry yeast

½ teaspoon cream of tartar

1 extra-large egg white

1⅔ cups warm water, about 100°F

1 extra-large egg, beaten with 1 tablespoon water (for egg wash)

1. Combine the flour, xanthan gum, sugar, salt, yeast, and cream of tartar in the bowl of your stand mixer. These are the dry ingredients. Line a baking sheet with parchment paper and set it aside.

2. Add the egg white to the dry ingredients and use your mixer's paddle attachment to combine. Add the warm water to the mixture. Begin by turning the mixer on low speed to allow the dry ingredients to begin to incorporate into the wet ingredients. Turn off the mixer, scrape down the bowl, and then turn the mixer back on, this time on a higher speed, and let it work for 6 to 7 minutes.

3. Divide the dough in half. Take one half and roll it between two large sheets of plastic wrap into a 10 x 8-inch rectangle. Remove the plastic wrap from one side of the dough, sprinkle with some extra flour, and replace the plastic wrap. Invert the dough, remove the other piece of plastic wrap, and sprinkle that side of the dough with some extra flour. Fold the two shorter sides of the dough to

meet in the middle. Pinch the opposite ends together to seal them, and turn the dough over so it is seam-side down. With well-floured hands, roll the dough back and forth to lengthen it to about 12 inches. Repeat this process with the other half of the dough.

4. Allow the loaves to rise in a warm, draft-free area for about 30 minutes, or until they have nearly doubled in volume (more or less, depending upon the temperature and humidity level at the time in your kitchen). Preheat your oven to 375°F. Once they are finished rising, place the two loaves about 2 inches apart on the lined baking sheet and make deep diagonal slashes every 2 inches along the length of each loaf. Brush the loaves with the egg wash using a pastry brush.

5. Place the loaves on the baking sheet in the center of the preheated oven for 20 to 25 minutes, or until golden brown. For a crispier crust, spray the loaves with water after 10 minutes of baking and then bake for the remaining 10 to 15 minutes.

6. Allow the bread to cool to room temperature before eating.

Shoestring Savings

French Bread

On a shoestring: $1.42 per baguette

If you bought it: $3.85 per baguette (frozen)

Cornmeal Flatbread

MAKES 4 SERVINGS OF FLATBREAD

When I make this flatbread, I generally use light coconut milk, since regular coconut milk has a tremendous amount of fat that I find gratuitous. You can easily substitute another liquid for the coconut milk altogether, but it must be something with some fat or you'll have a terrible time trying to remove it from the pan. And be sure to use a pan that is at least 10 inches in diameter, or the dough will be too thick and it just won't cook all the way through. Oh, and you have to be patient and let it bake, or the center will be gooey.

2 tablespoons extra-virgin olive oil

1 cup all-purpose gluten-free flour

½ teaspoon xanthan gum

½ cup cornmeal

½ teaspoon kosher salt

1 (14-ounce) can coconut milk (light or regular)

1. Preheat the oven to 400°F.
2. Pour the olive oil in an approximately 10-inch ovenproof skillet or pan. Place the skillet or pan in a hot oven for 3 minutes, until the oil is hot.
3. In medium bowl, whisk together the flour, xanthan gum, cornmeal, and salt. Make a well in the dry ingredients and pour in the coconut milk. Whisk to combine. The mixture should be the consistency of pancake batter.
4. Remove the skillet from the oven, pour the mixture into the bottom of the hot skillet, and return it to the oven.
5. Bake for 1 hour, until the flatbread is browned and firm to the touch. Remove from oven and allow the flatbread to chill out in the pan for a few minutes. Then slide it out, cut it into wedges, and serve right out of the oven, or at room temperature.

Focaccia

MAKES 1 FOCACCIA BREAD

My favorite way to serve focaccia is as an appetizer. Once it has been topped and baked, slice it into rectangles and serve it warm. You can top it however you like, or just brush it with some olive oil and rub it with some roasted garlic. I like to use chopped tomatoes and red onions tossed in a simple vinaigrette.

3½–4 cups all-purpose gluten-free flour

2 teaspoons xanthan gum

¼ teaspoon cream of tartar

2 tablespoons sugar

2 teaspoons active dry yeast

1 tablespoon kosher salt

½ teaspoon apple cider vinegar

1 extra-large egg white

1 cup warm water, about 100°F

4 tablespoons extra-virgin olive oil (plus more to coat dough while it rises)

1. In the bowl of your stand mixer fitted with the paddle attachment, combine the flour, xanthan gum, cream of tartar, sugar, yeast, and salt and mix to combine. Add the vinegar and egg white and mix on low speed to combine. With the mixer on low speed, add the water in a slow and steady stream. Once the dry ingredients have mostly incorporated into the wet ingredients, add the 4 tablespoons of olive oil. Then turn the mixer up to at least half throttle and mix for 6 to 8 minutes. This will activate the xanthan gum and allow it to do its job during rising.

2. Turn the dough out into a large bowl drizzled with a bit of olive oil, shaping the dough into a round with wet hands and turning it gently in the bowl to coat with the oil on all sides. Cover the bowl and place it in a warm, moist place to rise for 30 to 45 minutes until the dough has nearly doubled in size. The time it takes the dough to rise depends on the weather. It may take more time in cool, dry weather, or less time in warm, moist weather.

3. As the dough rises, preheat your oven to 400°F. Line a rimmed baking sheet with parchment paper. Turn the dough out onto the parchment paper, cover the top with plastic wrap, and start to roll it out. Stretch it to fill the baking sheet, edge to edge. Now you can dimple the dough with your finger, if you like. Brush the top of the bread with olive oil and whatever toppings you like. Since this is a doughy bread, rather than a pizza crust that you want to crisp, there is no need to blind bake it (where you would bake it plain before topping or filling it) before putting on toppings.

4. Place the baking sheet in the center of your preheated oven and bake for 15 to 20 minutes, or until the focaccia is lightly golden brown.

Shoestring Savings

Focaccia

On a shoestring: $3.77 for the entire bread

If you bought it: $16.47 for an equal amount
    (frozen)

Sourdough Bread

MAKES 1 LOAF

If baking bread is a labor of love, then baking sourdough bread is a labor of true romance. If you are searching for renewed inspiration to continue experimenting with different types of gluten-free bread, you might just find what are you looking for in the smell of the **Sourdough Starter** (page 46), how it improves with age. Picture it. One evening, you idly decide to open up the starter that has been lingering in the back of your refrigerator. You realize you were planning to make some bread the next day anyhow, so why not feed the starter, just in case you decide to take the leap and make sourdough bread. You awake the next morning, feeling that now-familiar sense of inspiration as you develop a greater and greater degree of mastery of gluten-free cooking and baking than you had assumed possible. You're so glad you decided to feed that starter "just in case." Today's the day the house will smell of fresh, homemade sourdough bread. Just follow my lead.

3 cups all-purpose gluten-free flour

2 teaspoons xanthan gum

¼ teaspoon cream of tartar

¼ cup sugar

1½ teaspoons kosher salt

2 teaspoons active dry yeast

1 cup "fed" **Sourdough Starter** (page 46)

3 tablespoons unsalted butter, melted and cooled

1½ cups warm milk (about 100°F)

1. Grease well a 9 x 5-inch loaf pan with unsalted butter and set it aside.

2. In the bowl of a stand mixer fitted with the paddle attachment, mix the flour, xanthan gum, cream of tartar, sugar, salt, and yeast to combine. Add the sourdough starter and butter and mix to combine.

3. With the mixer on low, pour in the milk in a slow, steady stream. Once the flour has begun to incorporate the liquids, beat the ingredients on at least

medium speed for 4 to 6 minutes. The dough will be pretty sticky—thicker than cake batter, not quite as thick as cookie dough. Scrape the dough into the greased loaf pan and smooth the top with wet hands.

4. Allow the dough to rise in a warm, damp place for 30 to 45 minutes, or until it has about doubled in size. In a colder, drier environment, this will take longer. If the environment is warm and humid, it may take less time. While the dough is rising, preheat the oven to 400°F.

5. Bake the loaf in the oven for 40 to 45 minutes, or until a nice, golden brown crust has formed on top.

Dinner Rolls

MAKES 15 TO 17 ROLLS

I don't usually make hamburger buns. There, I said it. I simply find that it's just not enough gluten-free bang for my hard-earned buck. I have been known to wrap a cooked hamburger in pizza dough, and bake it in a hot, 400-degree oven for 5 to 7 minutes, but hamburger rolls are thick and doughy. They just don't go far enough. And it's not like they're an eating experience all their own, like **Plain Bagels** (page 74), which I make regularly. Dinner rolls are a different story altogether. They're small, and they really do top off a meal quite nicely. A nice big plate of spaghetti and meatballs is taken to another level when you serve it with a beautifully browned roll on the side. And these rolls bake in rows and have to be pulled apart to serve. It's just so . . . satisfying.

1 stick (8 tablespoons) unsalted butter, melted and cooled

3½ cups all-purpose gluten-free flour, plus ¼ cup extra for dredging

2½ teaspoons xanthan gum

2 tablespoons sugar

½ teaspoon kosher salt

¼ teaspoon cream of tartar

2¼ teaspoons active dry yeast

1 extra-large egg white, at room temperature

2 cups warm water (about 100°F)

1 extra-large egg, beaten with 1 tablespoon water (for egg wash)

1. Line rimmed baking sheets with parchment paper and set them aside.

2. In the bowl of a stand mixer fitted with the paddle attachment, blend the butter until light and fluffy. Add the flour, xanthan gum, sugar, salt, cream of tartar, and yeast to the butter. Mix at low speed to allow the dry ingredients to begin to come together with the butter. Add the egg white and beat to combine. With the mixer still on low, add the water in a slow, steady stream. Once the dough has started to come together, turn the mixture up to at least half speed and beat

for about 6 minutes. Cover the mixture with a kitchen towel if necessary to avoid the escape of any bits of dough.

3. Divide the dough into 15–17 balls of dough with a 1½-inch wide ice cream scoop. Dredge the balls lightly in the extra ¼ cup flour and gently roll into proper balls in between your palms.

4. Place the rolls ¾ inch apart on the baking sheets. Allow them to rise in a warm, draft-free area for about 30 minutes, or until they've nearly doubled in volume (more or less, depending upon the temperature and humidity level at the time in your kitchen). Ideally, the rolls will be side by side, nearly touching. While the rolls are rising, preheat your oven to 375°F.

5. Using a pastry brush, brush the rolls with the egg wash. Bake for 20 to 25 minutes, until golden brown. Serve warm or at room temperature.

Shoestring Savings

Dinner Rolls

On a shoestring: 27¢ per roll.

If you bought it: $1.87 per roll (frozen)

Buttermilk Biscuits

MAKES 6 TO 8 BISCUITS

These beauties can be frozen after the dough is cut into rounds and then baked from frozen in a preheated, 450°F oven for about 20 minutes. It's best to freeze them first on a baking sheet, so they don't clump together, and then transfer them to a freezer-safe, resealable plastic bag. They're light and flaky and comforting any time of day, like a proper biscuit should be.

2 cups all-purpose gluten-free flour

1 teaspoon xanthan gum

1 tablespoon baking powder

½ teaspoon baking soda

2 tablespoons sugar

1 teaspoon kosher salt

1 stick (8 tablespoons) unsalted butter, diced and chilled

1 cup buttermilk (or 1 cup milk plus 1 tablespoon white wine vinegar, shaken)

1. Preheat your oven to 450°F. Line a rimmed baking sheet with parchment paper and set it aside.

2. In a large bowl, place the flour, xanthan gum, baking powder, baking soda, sugar, and salt and whisk to combine. Add the cold, diced butter to the large bowl with the dry ingredients. Using a handheld pastry blender (or simply two knives, or a food processor, if you prefer), cut the butter into the dry ingredients until the mixture resembles small peas.

3. Add the buttermilk and mix with a spoon (or pulse about three times if using a food processor) until the mixture begins to come together. Wrap the dough in plastic wrap, squeeze it a bit to press it together, and place in the refrigerator to chill for 15 to 20 minutes (or up to overnight).

4. Remove the dough from the refrigerator and use a rolling pin to flatten it into a proper disk that is approximately 1 inch thick. The dough should be mostly smooth and mostly round. A round shape will make easier work of cutting rounds of dough with a biscuit cutter.

5. Peel back the plastic wrap. If the dough seems too sticky, cover it again with the plastic wrap and place it back in the refrigerator for another spell of about 15 minutes. Once it is ready, with the plastic wrap peeled back, cut out rounds of dough with a floured 2½-inch round biscuit cutter. Roll the scraps up again, press into a mound, cover with plastic wrap, and have another go at it with the biscuit cutter. Conventional wisdom is only to re-roll scraps once, but that sticks in my (shoestring) craw. Re-roll to your heart's content. The last little bits can just be baked off in any shape you like.

6. Transfer rounds (and assorted scraps) to the baking sheet, spaced about 1 inch apart (or less—they won't spread during baking).

7. Place the sheets in the preheated oven and bake for 15 to 17 minutes, until puffy and pale golden. Rotate the sheets halfway through baking.

Shoestring Savings

Buttermilk Biscuits

On a shoestring: 45¢ per biscuit

If you bought it: $1.17 per biscuit (frozen)

Sweet Potato Biscuits

MAKES 6 TO 8 BISCUITS

These biscuits are a newer twist on an old favorite. Their beautiful golden color and sweet aroma never disappoint. Like the **Buttermilk Biscuits** (page 100), these can be placed 1 inch apart on a rimmed baking sheet and frozen before baking, and then stored in a freezer-safe bag until you're ready to use them. Just increase the baking time by about 5 minutes if you bake them from frozen or defrost them overnight in the refrigerator before using them.

2 cups all-purpose gluten-free flour

1 teaspoon xanthan gum

1 tablespoon baking powder

½ teaspoon baking soda

2 tablespoons sugar

1 teaspoon kosher salt

1 stick (8 tablespoons) unsalted butter, diced and chilled

¾ cup pureed baked sweet potatoes (about 2 medium sweet potatoes)

⅓ cup sour cream (low-fat is fine, nonfat is not)

¼ cup milk (low-fat is fine, nonfat is not)

1. Preheat your oven to 450°F. Line a rimmed baking sheet with parchment paper and set it aside.

2. In a large bowl, place the flour, xanthan gum, baking powder, baking soda, sugar, and salt and whisk to combine. Add the cold, diced butter to the large bowl with the dry ingredients. Using a handheld pastry blender (or simply two knives, or a food processor, if you prefer), cut the butter into the dry ingredients until the mixture resembles small peas. The idea is for the butter to be in small pieces, and each small piece to be surrounded by the flour mixture.

3. In a separate small bowl, place the sweet potatoes, sour cream, and milk and mix to combine. Add these ingredients to the large bowl and mix with a spoon (or pulse about three times if using a food processor) until the dough begins to come together. Wrap the dough in plastic wrap, press it together, and

place the dough in the refrigerator to chill for 15 to 20 minutes (or for as long as overnight).

4. Remove the dough from the refrigerator and use a rolling pin to flatten it into a proper disk that is nearly 1 inch thick. The dough should be mostly smooth and mostly round. A round shape will make easier work of cutting rounds of dough with a biscuit cutter.

5. Peel back the plastic wrap. If the dough seems too sticky, cover it again with the plastic wrap and place it back in the refrigerator for another spell of about 15 minutes. Once it is ready, with the plastic wrap peeled back, cut out rounds of dough with a floured 2½-inch round biscuit cutter. Roll the scraps up again, press into a mound, cover with plastic wrap, and have another go at it with the biscuit cutter. Re-roll to your heart's content. The last little bits can just be baked in any shape you like.

6. Transfer rounds (and assorted scraps) to the baking sheet, spaced about 1 inch apart or less (they won't spread during baking).

7. Place the sheets in the preheated oven and bake for 15 to 17 minutes, until puffy and golden. Rotate the sheets halfway through baking.

White Sandwich Bread

MAKES 1 LOAF

When I nailed the recipe for this bread, I knew lunch would never be the same again. As you can see in the photographs section of this book, this sandwich bread has a thick, bakery-style crust that makes a satisfying crunch when you bite into it. It's sturdy enough to stand up to any filling at all, and it doesn't need to be toasted to do it. Once it has cooled completely, it can also be sliced as thin as Melba toast, cut into rectangles, and served with cheese. Picture the sandwich you've been missing and know that the wait is over. The recipe calls for a loaf pan that is no more than 9 x 5 inches because gluten-free flours are heavier than conventional flour. A smaller loaf pan helps keep the dough stable during rising, and then during baking.

3 cups all-purpose gluten-free flour

2¼ teaspoons xanthan gum

2 teaspoons kosher salt

3¼ teaspoons active dry yeast

¼ teaspoon cream of tartar

2 tablespoons sugar

1½ cups warm milk (about 100°F)

¼ cup (4 tablespoons) butter, melted and cooled

1 teaspoon apple cider vinegar

2 extra-large egg whites, beaten

1. Combine flour, xanthan gum, salt, yeast, cream of tartar, and sugar in the bowl of your stand mixer. These are the dry ingredients.

2. Grease well a 9 x 5-inch loaf pan (or even slightly smaller) with unsalted butter, getting every crevice. Set that aside, too.

3. Add the butter, vinegar, egg whites, and milk to the dry ingredients one at a time, using your mixer's paddle attachment to mix well after each addition.

4. Begin by turning the mixer on low speed and give the dry ingredients a moment of slow dancing to incorporate into the wet ingredients. Scrape down

the sides of the mixer bowl if any ingredients are left out. The mixture should be thick and stiff and some of it should stick to the sides of the mixing bowl.

5. Once the dry ingredients have been combined with the wet ingredients, open that baby up. Turn the mixer to at least half throttle and mix for 6 to 8 minutes, covering the mixer with a kitchen towel in case any bits of batter fly out of the mixing bowl. This step activates the xanthan gum.

6. Scrape the dough into the prepared loaf pan. The dough should leave only about an inch to spare at the top of the loaf pan. Allow the dough in the pan to rise, covered, in a warm, humid, draft-free place for 30 to 45 minutes. It should be overflowing the top of the loaf pan by at least half an inch when you retrieve it but will not have doubled in volume. It may take longer to rise properly in colder, drier weather and less time in warmer, more humid weather.

7. While the dough is rising, preheat the oven to 375°F. Go by your oven thermometer, not your oven dial. (If you don't have an oven thermometer, get one!)

8. Bake in a properly preheated oven for 45 to 60 minutes. The outside will form a thick, brown crust. Allow to cool for about 10 minutes in the pan and then completely on a wire rack.

Shoestring Savings

White Sandwich Bread

On a shoestring: $3.63 per loaf

If you bought it: $8.00 per loaf

English Muffin Bread

MAKES 1 LOAF

This bread dough can also be divided before baking and placed into molds to make individual English muffins. Simply reduce the baking time to 30 to 40 minutes. Sprinkling it with cornmeal, whether it's made as a loaf or as muffins, is the finishing touch that lends this recipe its authentic feel.

3½ cups all-purpose gluten-free flour

2½ teaspoons xanthan gum

¼ teaspoon cream of tartar

1 tablespoon sugar

3¼ teaspoons active dry yeast

2 teaspoons kosher salt

¼ teaspoon baking soda

1 teaspoon apple cider vinegar

1 extra-large egg white

2 tablespoons canola oil

2 cups warm milk (about 100°F) (low-fat is fine, nonfat is not)

1 tablespoon cornmeal

1. In the bowl of your stand mixer fitted with the paddle attachment, combine the flour, xanthan gum, cream of tartar, sugar, yeast, salt, and baking soda. Add the vinegar, egg white, and canola oil and mix on low speed to combine. With the mixer on low speed, add the milk in a slow and steady stream. Once the dry ingredients have mostly incorporated into the wet ingredients, turn the mixer up to at least half throttle and mix for 6 to 8 minutes. This will activate the xanthan gum, and allow it to do its job during rising.

2. Grease well a loaf pan that is no larger than 9 x 5 inches with unsalted butter. When the dough has finished mixing, scrape it into the prepared loaf pan and place it in a warm, moist place to rise for 30 to 45 minutes until the dough has risen past the lip of the loaf pan. In cool, dry weather, the dough may take longer to rise; in warm, moist weather, it may take less time to rise.

3. While the dough is rising, preheat the oven to 375°F.

4. After the dough has risen, place the loaf pan in the center of the oven and bake for 45 to 55 minutes, or until pale golden and crusty on top. Cool for 5 minutes in the loaf pan and then turn out onto a wire rack to cool completely.

Brioche Bread

MAKES 1 LARGE LOAF

This brioche bread is a real treat. It's lightly sweet and rich with eggs and butter. It also has a super-thick golden crust and golden yellow softness inside. You'll find it makes the best French toast you've ever had, gluten-free or not, and even makes delicious sandwiches. All the eggs in this recipe make for a really puffy, stable loaf and also give this bread a long life in the refrigerator. The dough can also be used to make brioche rolls.

2½ cups all-purpose gluten-free flour

1¾ teaspoons xanthan gum

½ cup sugar

2½ teaspoons active dry yeast

1 teaspoon cream of tartar

¾ teaspoon kosher salt

1 teaspoon grated lemon zest

½ teaspoon apple cider vinegar

5 extra-large eggs, at room temperature

½ cup warm milk, about 100°F (low-fat is fine, nonfat is not)

1 stick plus 2 tablespoons (10 tablespoons) unsalted butter, at room temperature

1. In the bowl of your stand mixer fitted with the paddle attachment, place the flour, xanthan gum, sugar, yeast, cream of tartar, and salt and mix on low speed to combine.

2. To the bowl of dry ingredients, add the lemon zest, vinegar, and eggs and mix on low speed to combine. With the mixer on low speed, add the milk in a slow and steady stream. Once the dry ingredients have mostly incorporated into the wet ingredients, with the mixer still on low speed, add the butter one tablespoon at a time. Once all the butter has been added, turn the mixer up to at least half throttle and mix for 6 to 8 minutes to activate the xanthan gum.

3. Preheat the oven to 375°F. Grease well a 9 x 5-inch loaf pan with unsalted butter. Brioche has so many eggs that it rises quite a lot, so even a pan that is

slightly larger than this will work well. When the dough has finished mixing, scrape it into the prepared loaf pan and place it in a warm, moist place to rise for 30 to 45 minutes until the dough has risen past the lip of the loaf pan. In cool, dry weather, the dough may take longer to rise; in warm, moist weather, it may take less time to rise.

4. After the dough has risen, place the loaf pan in the center of the preheated oven and bake for 20 minutes. Then cut a slash down the center of the bread to allow steam to escape, and tent the loaf with foil. Bake 20 to 25 minutes more, or until golden brown with a thick crust on top. Cool for 15 minutes in the loaf pan and then turn out onto a wire rack to cool completely.

Irish Soda Bread

MAKES 1 LARGE LOAF

We have no family connection at all to Ireland, but I always tell my children that they can celebrate any holiday they like. They always want to celebrate St. Patrick's Day by eating Irish Soda Bread. I'm beginning to think that they're just in it for the food, though, and I'm not entirely sure that alone qualifies as celebrating. Irish Soda Bread is a little different than most other quick breads. It's made with baking soda and baking powder, like other quick breads, but it's traditionally not baked in a loaf pan, and the dough is firmer than you might expect.

3 cups all-purpose gluten-free flour

1½ teaspoons xanthan gum

¾ cup sugar

2¼ teaspoons baking powder

1 teaspoon baking soda

½ teaspoon kosher salt

¼ teaspoon cream of tartar

6 tablespoons unsalted butter, diced and chilled

2 cups raisins (good ones, like Thompsons, are not much more expensive and are worth it)

2 tablespoons caraway seeds (optional)

1½ cups milk (low-fat is fine, nonfat is not)

2 teaspoons white wine vinegar

1 extra-large egg

1. Preheat the oven to 350°F. Grease a 10- or 12-inch ovenproof skillet with sides 2 inches or higher with unsalted butter and set it aside.

2. In a large bowl, place the flour, xanthan gum, sugar, baking powder, baking soda, salt, and cream of tartar. Whisk to combine.

3. Place the cold, diced butter into the large bowl with the dry ingredients. Using a handheld pastry blender (or simply two knives, or a food processor, if you prefer), cut the butter into the dry ingredients until the mixture resembles small peas. The idea is for the butter to be in small pieces, and each small piece

to be surrounded by the flour mixture. Stir in the raisins and (optional) caraway seeds.

4. Add the milk, vinegar, and egg and mix with a spoon (or pulse about three times if using a food processor) until the mixture begins to come together.

5. Scrape the dough into the prepared ovenproof skillet, and, with wet hands, smooth the top of the dough, piling it a bit higher in the center and pulling it about ⅛ inch away from the edges of the skillet. With a sharp knife, cut a deep "X" into the center of the dough.

6. Place the skillet into the preheated oven and bake for 40 minutes. Turn down the oven temperature to 325°F and bake for another 30 to 35 minutes, or until a toothpick inserted into the center comes out completely clean. Allow the bread to cool in the pan for about 30 minutes and then turn onto a wire rack to cool completely.

7. Strike up the band, Danny Boy, and begin your gluten-free St. Patrick's Day celebration, Irish or not!

Potato Bread

MAKES 1 LOAF

Moist and flavorful, this potato bread is a bit more delicate than the **White Sandwich Bread** (page 104). If you ever find yourself making mashed potatoes, perhaps as an ingredient in **Shepherd's Pie** (page 164), just make ½ cup extra and set it aside to make some potato bread. Even better, make a bunch of mashed potatoes, serve some as a side for dinner, then set some aside to make potato bread, Shepherd's Pie, and **Potato Gnocchi** (page 126). That's some nice piggybacking, indeed.

3 cups all-purpose gluten-free flour

2¼ teaspoons xanthan gum

¼ teaspoon cream of tartar

2 tablespoons sugar

3¼ teaspoons active dry yeast

1 teaspoon kosher salt

1 teaspoon apple cider vinegar

1 extra-large egg white

7 tablespoons unsalted butter, at room temperature

½ cup sour cream (low-fat is fine, nonfat is not)

½ cup mashed potatoes (red-skin, yellow-skin, or Idaho potatoes, boiled, peeled, and mashed)

1 cup warm water (about 100°F)

1. In the bowl of your stand mixer fitted with the paddle attachment, combine the flour, xanthan gum, cream of tartar, sugar, yeast, and salt. Add the vinegar, egg white, butter, sour cream, and mashed potatoes, mixing on low speed in between additions to combine. With the mixer on low speed, add the water in a slow and steady stream. Once the dry ingredients have mostly been incorporated into the wet ingredients, turn the mixer up to at least half throttle and mix for 6 to 8 minutes. This will activate the xanthan gum and allow it to do its job during rising.

2. Preheat the oven to 375°F. Grease well a loaf pan that is no larger than 9 x 5 inches with unsalted butter. When the dough has finished mixing, scrape the dough into the prepared loaf pan and place it in a warm, moist place to rise for 30 to 45 minutes until the dough has risen past the lip of the loaf pan. In cool, dry weather, the dough may take longer to rise; in warm, moist weather, it may take less time to rise.

3. After the dough has risen, place the loaf pan in the center of the preheated oven and bake for 40 to 50 minutes, or until pale golden. Cool for 5 minutes in the loaf pan, and then turn out onto a wire rack to cool completely.

Seeded Bagels

MAKES 10 REGULAR-SIZE (NOT JUMBO) BAGELS

I never got the whole concept of the "everything" bagel. In my experience, you *can* in fact have everything in life, just not generally all at once. Then again, to each his own. Who am I to judge if you want to try to have it all—all at once? Me, I stick with one type of seed at a time, so I can enjoy each one in its own right. But that's just how I roll (or bagel, as the case may be). If you want to do all the seeds at once, go for it. Carpe bagel.

4 cups all-purpose gluten-free flour (plus extra for dusting)

3 teaspoons xanthan gum

1 tablespoon kosher salt

1 tablespoon active dry yeast

6 tablespoons honey

2–3 cups warm water (about 100°F)

2 tablespoons sugar

1 extra-large egg, beaten with 1 tablespoon water (for egg wash)

½ cup seeds (sesame, poppy, caraway, etc.)

1. In a large bowl, place the flour, xanthan gum, salt, and yeast and whisk to combine. To the dry ingredients, add the honey and mix to distribute. It will sort of clump a bit, and that's fine.

2. In a slow but steady stream, add 2 cups of the water, mixing with a spoon as you pour. Mix until the dough begins to come together. If it is not coming together, add more water a bit at a time, mixing as you go, until it comes together. The dough should be thick and sticky, but not impossible to handle. Divide the dough into ten heaped portions, sprinkling each portion with a light dusting of flour and rolling it gently between the palms of your hands into a disk about 1¼ inches thick. With a well-floured index finger, create a small hole in the center of each disk. Move your finger in a gentle circular motion to widen the hole. Turn the disk over and repeat the procedure on the other side.

3. Place the mounds of dough about 1 inch apart on a rimmed baking sheet lined with parchment paper and allow them to rise in a warm, moist place for 30 to 45 minutes until the dough has risen to about 1½ times its original size. In cool, dry weather, the dough may take longer to rise; in warm, moist weather, it may take less time to rise.

4. While the bagels are rising, boil a pot or pan full of water, at least 6 inches deep. Dissolve the sugar in the boiling water. After the bagels have risen, gently place the mounds of dough into the boiling water, two at a time, for 3 minutes total. Gently turn over the bagels halfway through boiling.

5. As they finish boiling, place each bagel on the parchment paper–lined baking sheets, about 1 inch apart. With a pastry brush, brush each bagel generously with the egg wash. Sprinkle the bagels all over with your seeds of choice.

6. At this point, the bagels can be frozen on the baking sheets until solid, then placed in freezer-safe resealable plastic bags to be baked another time. They should be thawed for at least 2 hours at room temperature before baking (or you can stick them in the "defrost" mode in your microwave for a bit for a quick defrost, but you'll be a little sad if you do that since they won't turn out quite as good).

7. Once you are ready to bake them, preheat the oven to 375°F. Place the bagels about 1 inch apart on the parchment paper–lined rimmed baking sheets in the preheated oven and bake them for about 25 minutes, or until they are golden brown.

8. Allow the bagels to cool at least 15 to 20 minutes before slicing them open.

Soft Pretzels

MAKES 10 TO 12 LARGE SOFT PRETZELS

This pretzel dough is remarkably similar to pizza dough, except it omits the olive oil. And the dough is dipped in a baking soda bath before you bake it. My Philadelphia-born husband won't admit it, but these taste just like the soft pretzels they sell all over Philly. Yum.

2 cups all-purpose gluten-free flour

1½ teaspoons xanthan gum

1 tablespoon active dry yeast

2 teaspoons light brown sugar

¾ teaspoon kosher salt

¾ to 1 cup warm water (about 100°F)

1–2 tablespoons vegetable oil

2 cups warm water (about 100°F) plus 2 tablespoons baking soda (for baking soda bath)

1. In a medium-size bowl, place the flour, xanthan gum, yeast, sugar, and salt and stir to combine.

2. To the flour mixture, add ¾ cup of water in a steady stream and either pulse in a food processor or mix in a bowl with a spoon or fork to combine. If you are using a food processor, pulse while streaming in the water, until a ball begins to form. Otherwise, stir constantly while streaming in the water and continue stirring until the mixture begins to come together. If the dough is not coming together, add as much of the final ¼ cup of water as necessary. If the dough seems super sticky, add some more flour a tablespoon at a time and stir or pulse to combine. Press the dough into a disk.

3. Place the dough in another medium-size bowl and drizzle it with the oil, turning the dough it to coat it. Cover the bowl with plastic wrap and place it in a warm, draft-free area to rise until it has doubled in volume (about 1 hour).

4. After the dough has risen, wrap it in plastic wrap and chill it for at least an hour.

5. Once the dough has chilled, make the baking soda bath by combining the 2 cups warm water and baking soda in an 8-inch square pan. Preheat your oven to 450°F. Line rimmed baking sheets with parchment paper and set them aside.

6. Take the chilled dough and cut it into 10 to 12 pieces with kitchen shears or a sharp knife. With wet hands, roll each piece of dough into a cylinder that is about 2 feet long and about ½ inch thick. Twist the dough into a pretzel shape, dip it into the baking bath, and place it on the prepared baking sheets. Repeat with the remaining pieces of dough.

7. Place the baking sheets in the center of the preheated oven and bake until golden brown, 8 to 10 minutes.

Shoestring Savings

Soft Pretzels

On a shoestring: 17¢ per pretzel

If you bought it: $2.00 per pretzel (frozen)

Flour Tortillas

MAKES 6 TORTILLAS. IT CAN BE DOUBLED EASILY.

For far too long, I used commercially prepared corn tortillas whenever I made burritos, quesadillas, and anything in between. I figured gluten-free flour tortillas were going to be way more trouble than they were worth. Boy was I wrong. They have precious few ingredients, and I even make them in a dry cast-iron skillet, so there's little cleanup. It's nice to have an authentic burrito now and then. It makes a great lunchbox item for my kids, too.

2 cups all-purpose gluten-free flour
1 teaspoon xanthan gum
1½ teaspoons baking powder
1 teaspoon kosher salt
4 teaspoons vegetable oil
1 cup warm water, about 100°F

1. In a large bowl, place the flour, xanthan gum, baking powder, and salt and mix to combine well. Add the vegetable oil and stir to combine. Add the water in a slow, steady stream, stirring to combine as you pour.

2. Once you have finished adding the water, press together the dough with wet hands. Divide into six pieces. Roll each piece separately between two sheets of plastic wrap until about ⅛ inch thick and about 8 inches wide.

3. Heat a large cast-iron (or nonstick) skillet. Once the skillet is hot, one at a time, place each raw tortilla flat in the skillet. Allow each to cook for 45 to 60

Shoestring Savings

Flour Tortillas

On a shoestring: $1.62 for 6 tortillas
If you bought it: $3.19 for 6 tortillas (frozen)

seconds, or until slightly charred on the underside. You're better off under-cooking them than over-cooking. If you burn them, they won't be pliable. Then, with a large, heatproof spatula, flip the tortilla and cook for another 30 to 45 seconds. Remove each from the pan and place on a plate.

4. These are best used when they're still warm. If they stiffen a bit upon standing, just microwave them for 30 seconds surrounded by a moistened paper towel. They'll be good as new.

Popovers

MAKES 6 LARGE, OR 12 SMALL, POPOVERS

If you've never had popovers, you've been missing out. Crusty on top, almost pudding-like at the very bottom, popovers are super easy to make, require very few ingredients, and you can even use a plain old muffin tin. Although using a special popover pan does make a more beautiful presentation, and the spacing between the cups helps them to puff, you can live your whole life without a popover pan very nicely, thank you.

1 cup all-purpose gluten-free flour

½ teaspoon xanthan gum

½ teaspoon kosher salt

1 tablespoon unsalted butter, melted and cooled

2 extra-large eggs, lightly beaten, at room temperature

1 cup milk (low-fat is fine, nonfat is not), at room temperature

1. Preheat the oven to 400°F. Grease well a 6-cup popover pan (or a regular muffin tin, if you don't have a popover pan) with unsalted butter and set it aside.

2. In a large bowl, whisk together the flour, xanthan gum, and salt. Add the butter, eggs, and milk, whisking well after each addition until the batter is smooth. The batter will be thin.

3. Fill each of the wells in the pan just under halfway full. Place the pan in the center of the preheated oven and bake for a total of 30 minutes. After the first 20 minutes, with a sharp knife or with sharp kitchen shears, pierce the top of each popover to allow steam to escape so that the popovers are able to maintain their puffiness.

4. Serve plain or with your favorite jam or preserves.

Six

Eat Your Vegetables: Vegetarian Meals and Sides

Baked Eggplant Parmesan

SERVES 4 PEOPLE AS A MAIN DISH OR 6 AS A SIDE DISH

This recipe makes a traditional layered eggplant Parmesan. But if you're feeling adventuresome or you're simply tight on time, it can be streamlined by peeling the eggplant, and then cutting it into a large dice rather than slicing it. This way, rather than carefully coating each individual eggplant slice in egg and then breadcrumbs, you can simply toss the diced eggplant first in the egg mixture, sprinkle with the breadcrumbs, and bake on a rimmed baking sheet in a single layer until the eggplant is soft and the breadcrumbs are beginning to crisp. Then proceed mostly as indicated below, layering the tomato sauce, baked eggplant, and cheese and baking as directed.

Either way, it's delicious, much less messy and less time consuming than frying the eggplant before layering and baking, and considerably healthier.

1 large or 2 medium eggplants, peeled and sliced in ¾-inch thick rounds

2–3 cups gluten-free breadcrumbs

2 extra-large eggs, beaten with ¼ cup milk and ¼ cup water

2–3 cups tomato sauce

10–12 ounces grated mozzarella cheese (more if you like)

1. Preheat your oven to 400°F. Line rimmed baking sheets with parchment paper and set them aside.

2. Place the egg mixture in wide, flat dish; place the breadcrumbs in another. Place one slice of raw eggplant in the egg mixture, invert it to coat the other side, and allow the excess to drip off. Next, press both sides of the eggplant firmly into the breadcrumbs and transfer to a prepared baking sheet. Repeat with the remaining slices of eggplant, arranging them 1 inch apart on the baking sheets.

3. Place the baking sheets in the preheated oven and bake until soft to the touch and golden brown, 15 to 20 minutes. Halfway through baking, flip the slices so they brown evenly on both sides.

4. While the eggplant is baking, grease a 9 x 12-inch baking dish with unsalted butter and spoon just enough tomato sauce into the pan to cover the bottom with a thin layer. Once the eggplant is done baking, remove the baking sheets from the oven and allow the eggplant to cool for 5 minutes, or even less. This allows the eggplant to become somewhat firm. Lower the oven temperature to 350°F.

5. Place one layer of eggplant over the layer of tomato sauce, cover each slice with sauce, and top generously with grated cheese. Continue with another layer of eggplant slices, sauce, and grated cheese, followed by one final layer.

6. Place the baking dish in the center of the oven and bake for 15 to 20 minutes until the cheese is melted and the sauce is bubbling.

Corn and Zucchini Fritters

MAKES 6 SERVINGS

I don't know about you, but where I live, zucchini are about the easiest, most foolproof things to grow in a home garden. They are hearty and they are prolific, two attributes I personally am not known for. And they make such beautiful, edible flowers. (I can't do that, either.) I love to cook 'em with some oil, chopped onion, and chopped canned tomatoes. And zucchini really do shine when you fry them up into fritters with some flour, butter, whole kernels of corn, and a few other basic pantry items.

1 extra-large egg, beaten
½ cup milk (low-fat is fine, nonfat is not)
2 tablespoons unsalted butter, melted and cooled
1 cup all-purpose gluten-free flour
½ teaspoon xanthan gum
1 teaspoon baking powder
½ teaspoon kosher salt
¼ teaspoon sugar
10 ounces frozen corn kernels (or two ears of fresh corn, boiled until tender, then cut from the ear)
2 medium zucchinis, grated and squeezed dry
Vegetable oil, for frying

1. In a large bowl, add the egg, milk, and butter and beat until well combined. Add the flour, xanthan gum, baking powder, salt, and sugar and mix until blended. Gently stir in the corn kernels, still frozen, and the grated zucchini.

2. In a heavy pot with at least 3-inch sides, heat about ¼ inch vegetable oil over medium high heat until it shimmers. Drop the fritter batter by heaping tablespoons into the hot oil and fry it until it turns golden brown, about 3 to 4 minutes total, turning over the fritters once during frying.

3. Gently remove the fritters from the oil and drain on plates lined with paper towels. Serve immediately.

Potato Gnocchi

MAKES 4 SERVINGS

For the sake of sanity (which I highly prize and find to be in short supply), I suggest that you complete Step 1 of this recipe, baking and mashing the potatoes, in advance. Whenever you're using the oven for something else already, bake the potatoes and keep them in the refrigerator until you are ready to use them. Many recipes for gnocchi call for boiling the potatoes. I think that is just silly. They absorb too much moisture, and then you have a heck of a time combating the extra moisture in the final product. If you bake them in a dry, hot oven, you will have them just where you want them.

The recipe below assumes that you have no chilled mashed potatoes on hand. But just think of how good it would feel to be able to skip right to Step 2. Since this recipe can be easily doubled, I often do just that and then, without boiling them, freeze half the gnocchi on a baking sheet in a single layer before putting them in a resealable freezer-safe storage bag. No need to defrost the dumplings before boiling them when you're ready to use them. Just boil them right out of the freezer.

4 large russet (or similar size) potatoes
2 tablespoons unsalted butter, melted and cooled
1 cup all-purpose gluten-free flour
½ teaspoon xanthan gum
½ teaspoon kosher salt

1. Preheat your oven to 400°F. Wash, pierce, and bake the potatoes in their skins for about an hour, until they're soft when you squeeze them. Let them cool slightly, then peel them. I use a vegetable peeler, but a carefully wielded sharp knife will do. Place the skinned potatoes in a large bowl, add the butter, and then beat them until they're very smooth. It is worth your time to use a food processor or a handheld or stand mixer to mash the potatoes until they're smooth. Place the mashed potatoes in the refrigerator to chill for at least 30 minutes.

2. Once the potatoes are chilled, add the flour, xanthan gum, and salt to the potatoes, kneading the dry ingredients into the potatoes, squeezing the dough as you go. It should hold together.

3. Now it's time to roll the dough into ropes. Roll lumps of dough into ropes that are about 3 to 6 inches long, or as long as you can manage them. Give each lump of dough a good squeeze in between your palms, and then roll the dough either between your palms or on a floured flat surface. The most important thing is that the dough holds together solidly. After you have rolled a few ropes, let them sit for a few minutes. It will allow the flour mixture to absorb the moisture of the potatoes.

4. While the dough is sitting, boil a large pot of water. In the meantime, cut the ropes into 1-inch pieces with a sharp knife, then mark each with the tines of a fork to make ridges (which will allow the gnocchi to hold on to sauce better). One by one (and in batches of about twenty), gently drop each little nugget into the boiling water and allow them to cook for about 3 minutes, until they float to the top (and it's very, very exciting when they do float to the top). Fish out the gnocchi with a slotted spoon and set them aside. Repeat this process with the remaining dough.

5. Serve gnocchi with tomato sauce (or whatever else you like).

Shoestring Savings

Potato Gnocchi

On a shoestring: $2.13 for 4 servings

If you bought it: $6.50 for 4 servings (frozen)

Ricotta Gnocchi

MAKES 4 SERVINGS

Compared to **Potato Gnocchi** (page 126), Ricotta Gnocchi are simpler to make because you are spared that first step of baking, peeling, and cooling the potatoes. Just like potato gnocchi dough, ricotta gnocchi dough must hold together firmly or it will fall apart during boiling. When in doubt, stick the dough in the refrigerator, as it will become firmer as it chills. This is unfortunately one of those recipes, though, where nondairy substitutes will just not work.

1¼ cups all-purpose gluten-free flour
½ teaspoon xanthan gum
½ teaspoon kosher salt
1 cup finely grated Parmesan cheese
16 ounces ricotta cheese (part skim or whole milk), kept chilled until ready to use

1. In a large bowl, whisk together the flour, xanthan gum, salt, and Parmesan cheese until well combined. Remove the ricotta cheese from the refrigerator right before you are ready to use it. Add the ricotta a bit at a time to the flour mixture and knead it in, squeezing the dough as you go. It should hold together.

2. As in the recipe for Potato Gnocchi, roll lumps of dough into ropes that are about 3 to 6 inches long. Give each lump of dough a good squeeze in between your palms and then roll the dough either between your palms or on a floured, flat surface until it holds together solidly. After you have rolled a few, allow them to sit for a few minutes so the flour mixture can absorb the moisture of the ricotta cheese. Add more flour if necessary.

3. While the dough is sitting, boil a large pot of salted water. In the meantime, cut the ropes into 1-inch pieces with a sharp knife, then mark each with the tines of a fork to make ridges (it allows the gnocchi to hold on to sauce better). One by one (and in batches of about twenty), gently drop each little nugget into the boiling water and allow them to cook for about 3 minutes, until they float to the top. Remove the gnocchi from the water with a slotted spoon and set them aside. Repeat with the remaining dough. Serve with tomato sauce (or whatever else you like).

Lentil Sloppy Joes

THIS RECIPE CAN BE EATEN AS A SANDWICH IN A ROLL OR EATEN IN
A BOWL WITH A SPOON. IF EATEN ON A ROLL, IT WILL SERVE 6 PEOPLE.
EATEN STRAIGHT UP WITH A SPOON, THE RECIPE SERVES 4.

My husband and I love these Lentil Sloppy Joes, which are nearly identical to the traditional beef version—although my children, for the most part, refuse to eat this. But I'm convinced that it's only because they made a pact in a former life that they would reject lentils for all eternity. There is no other reason that makes sense to me. To serve the sloppy Joes, you can use buns made from **Dinner Rolls** (page 98) that are a bit larger than called for in that recipe. The mixture is also delicious in a bowl with a dinner roll riding shotgun.

2 medium yellow onions, chopped

2 tablespoons vegetable oil

Kosher salt and freshly ground black pepper, to taste

1½ cups dried lentils

2½ cups tomato sauce

3–4 cups **Vegetable Stock** (see page 131)

2/ 3 cup packed light brown sugar

3–4 tablespoons Worcestershire Sauce

2–3 cups cooked brown rice

1. In a large stockpot, sauté the onions in the oil over medium heat until the onions are translucent, about 6 to 7 minutes. Add salt and pepper to taste. Add the lentils, tomato sauce, 3 cups of the Vegetable Stock, brown sugar, and Worcestershire sauce to the pan. Stir to dissolve the sugar and combine the rest of the ingredients. Bring the pot to a boil over medium-high heat. Reduce the heat to a simmer, cover, and cook for about 30 minutes, until the lentils are tender.

2. Once the lentils are tender, uncover the pot, add the rice and stir to combine. Continue to cook, uncovered, for about another 10 to 15 minutes, until the mixture reduces and thickens. It will thicken more as it cools. If necessary, you can add more Vegetable Stock to achieve the right consistency.

Polenta Pizza

MAKES 4 SERVINGS

I feel like I'm cheating on this one. It's really more of a concept than a recipe. The idea is that, for the purpose of staving off boredom (yours and that of your cooking audience), you make a quick batch of polenta, press it into the bottom of a springform pan, and make it into pizza by baking it with toppings of your choice. Then slice it into wedges and serve. If you are patient enough to wait for the polenta crust to brown, it will be a crispy delight that you can really sink your teeth into.

1¼ cups **Vegetable Stock** (see page 131)
1¼ cups milk (low-fat is fine, nonfat is not)
2 tablespoons unsalted butter
1 teaspoon kosher salt
1¼ cups coarse yellow cornmeal
2–3 tablespoons extra-virgin olive oil, for brushing
Sauce and cheese toppings of your choosing

1. Grease a 9-inch springform pan with unsalted butter and set it aside. Preheat your oven to 400°F.

2. In a medium saucepan, bring the stock, milk, butter, and salt to a boil over medium-high heat. Lower the heat to a simmer and add the cornmeal, whisking constantly. It will come together suddenly. Remove the saucepan from the heat and immediately spread the mixture on the bottom of the springform pan. With wet hands, push the polenta into the edges of the pan to create a raised edge. Brush the olive oil over the polenta crust. This will help it to brown in the oven.

3. Place the pan in the center of the preheated oven and bake for about 15 minutes, or until the crust is a bit browned. Remove it from the oven and top the polenta with some tomato sauce and some cheese, or whatever else you like, in whatever way you like. It can stand up to pretty much any topping.

4. Return the dish to the hot oven and bake for another 5 minutes, or until the cheese has melted. Allow the pizza to cool in the pan for approximately 5

minutes before popping off the sides of the springform pan and transferring the pizza to a flat surface. Slice the pie into 8 wedges with a large serrated knife. Serve immediately.

Vegetable Stock is so easy to make. In a large pot, combine a medium-size onion that you have peeled and sliced in half, a few cloves of garlic that have been crushed and peeled, a root vegetable (like sweet potatoes and/or parsnip), peeled and chopped, some whole carrots, peeled and chopped, and a few stalks of chopped celery. Add enough water to cover the vegetables, then add another inch of water, season liberally with kosher salt and freshly ground black pepper; cover the pot, bring the water to a boil, and simmer for about 45 minutes to an hour.

Spinach and Cheese Ravioli

MAKES ABOUT 12 RAVIOLI

The only special equipment you really need to make ravioli is a metal ravioli cutter. It cuts and seals the ravioli all in one motion and costs only a couple dollars at any good kitchen supply store (or on the Internet). But you don't need fancy mats and rolling pins to roll out the pasta; the rest of your regular equipment will do (until you open that Italian restaurant, of course.)

1 recipe **Fresh Gluten-Free Pasta Dough** (page 43)
1 cup frozen chopped spinach, thawed
2 teaspoons canola oil
1 tablespoon sea salt
1½ cups ricotta cheese
¼ cup fresh grated Parmesan cheese
¼ cup grated mozzarella cheese
2 tablespoons chopped fresh basil
1 extra-large egg, beaten
Kosher salt and freshly ground black pepper, to taste
1 extra-large egg, beaten with 1 tablespoon water (for egg wash)

1. Divide the fresh pasta dough into four equal portions and roll each portion between two sheets of plastic wrap into a rectangle ⅛ inch thick (the thickness of a nickel). Set aside the dough.

2. Place the spinach in a clean kitchen towel and wring out all the liquid. Begin to boil a large pot of water. Once the water is boiling, add the oil and sea salt. The salt will help to flavor the pasta, and the oil will help to keep the ravioli from sticking together during boiling.

3. While the water is coming to a boil, in a large bowl, combine the ricotta cheese, Parmesan cheese, mozzarella cheese, basil, and spinach and mix until well blended. Add the beaten egg and the salt and pepper to taste and mix to combine. In a separate small bowl, beat the egg and water together for the egg wash and set it aside.

4. Slice each rectangle of pasta dough into strips that are slightly wider than the width of your ravioli cutter. Gently score each strip of pasta dough with the ravioli cutter to help you approximate where to put the filling.

5. Place a tablespoon of filling in the center of each scored ravioli in one strip of pasta. Brush the egg wash on all of the exposed areas along the strip of dough that are not covered by the filling. This will seal the raviolis closed. Gently place another strip of pasta squarely over the top of the first strip, pressing between ravioli. Using the ravioli cutter, cut and seal each ravioli by positioning the cutter where the dough was scored, pressing down firmly, and popping the ravioli out of the cutter with your index finger. Repeat the process with the remaining dough and filling.

6. Divide the ravioli into two batches. Place the first batch into the large pot of boiling water. Return the water to boiling. Cooking times will depend somewhat upon the size of the ravioli, but should range from 6 to 8 minutes from the time the water begins to boil again. The ravioli are generally done once they have begun to swell in size a bit. Repeat with the second batch.

7. Gently remove the ravioli from the water and serve immediately with sauce. Do not rinse the ravioli or the sauce will not cling to them.

Spinach Pie

MAKES ONE 9-INCH SPINACH PIE

I love this dish for brunch as a great alternative to quiche. Serve it with some fresh fruit or some fluffy scrambled eggs. Or, add some tomato sauce to the spinach mixture, and it becomes more of a Mediterranean pizza, and dinner is ready to go. The olive oil crust can be made ahead of time, but because it does not contain yeast, and therefore doesn't have to rise, it can be ready in a flash anyhow.

1 recipe **Savory Olive Oil Crust** (page 42)

2 cloves garlic

1 medium red onion, chopped

2 tablespoons extra-virgin olive oil

1 pound frozen chopped spinach, thawed

4 ounces (about 1 cup) grated mozzarella cheese

2 ounces (about ½ cup) grated Parmesan cheese

4 ounces feta cheese, crumbled

1. Line a rimmed baking sheet with parchment paper and set it aside. Separate the olive oil crust into two equal portions. Place one portion between two sheets of plastic wrap and roll into a round about 10 inches in diameter. Repeat with the other portion. Place both olive oil crusts, still between sheets of plastic wrap, flat on a shelf in the refrigerator to chill for 10 to 15 minutes.

2. While the crust is chilling, make the filling. On a flat surface, place each clove of garlic beneath the flat of a wide knife and apply pressure to crush the clove. Remove the skin and place the whole crushed cloves of garlic, along with the onion and olive oil, in a small skillet. Sauté the garlic and onion in the oil until the onion is translucent and the garlic is fragrant, about 6 minutes. Spoon the onions and oil in a large bowl. Discard the garlic. Place the spinach in a clean kitchen towel and wring out all the liquid. Once the spinach is dry, add it to the onion mixture and mix to combine the ingredients. Add the three cheeses to the onion mixture and mix well to combine thoroughly.

3. Take both crusts from the refrigerator. Preheat your oven to 350°F. Remove the plastic wrap from one round of dough and place it, flat, on the prepared baking sheet. Spoon the spinach mixture onto the center of the dough on the baking sheet and spread it out evenly over the surface of the dough, leaving a 1-inch border all around. From the other round of dough, remove one sheet of plastic wrap and place it, exposed side down, on top of the spinach mixture and squarely atop the bottom crust. Carefully remove the remaining piece of plastic wrap from the top crust. Cinch together the edges of the top and bottom crusts all along the perimeter of the pie. With a very sharp knife, slice three to four vents into the top of the crust to allow steam to escape during baking.

4. Place the pie on the baking sheet and bake in the center of the oven for about 30 minutes, or until nicely browned all over.

5. Once the pie has finished baking, remove it from the baking sheet and place on a cutting board. With a large serrated knife, slice the pie into wedges and serve immediately.

Arepas

MAKES 10 TO 12 AREPAS

Arepas are baked or fried cornmeal cakes that are popular in Colombia and Venezuela. They're usually served split in half and filled with something yummy, like eggs and salsa. To make them, you will need precooked cornmeal. The quintessential brand is Harina PAN, but it can be hard to find. Where I live, Goya's version seems to be a bit easier to find; I have used both. Be particularly mindful of freshness dates when you buy these products or other dry grains or flours.

Making arepas is more art than science. I have tried to make the process as transparent as possible in these directions, but there is no substitute for experience. Just keep in mind that even when they do not become puffy because there's a crack you didn't seal, they still taste delicious. And practice makes perfect.

1 cup precooked cornmeal flour
1 cup grated mozzarella cheese
⅛ teaspoon kosher salt
1 cup plus 2–4 tablespoons tepid water
¼ cup vegetable oil

1. In a large bowl, combine the cornmeal flour, cheese, and salt. Add 1 cup of water and stir to combine and incorporate the water into the flour mixture. Add more water by the tablespoonful if necessary for the dough to come together. Once the dough has come together, cover the bowl with plastic wrap and allow it to stand at room temperature for 3 to 4 minutes. The cornmeal flour will continue to absorb water, and the dough will stiffen as it stands.

2. After the dough has stiffened, wet your hands and divide the dough into 10 to 12 portions of about 3 tablespoons each. With wet hands again, form the first piece of dough into a ball, then flatten into a disk about ¼ inch thick and 2½ inches wide. Repeat with each piece of dough.

3. Pour the oil into a 12-inch skillet with at least 2-inch high sides, and heat the oil over medium-high heat until it shimmers. While the oil heats, prepare

the first portion of dough for frying. Wet your hands again and press all around the edge of the disk, eliminating any cracks. Flatten along the side, smoothing as you go. When you fry the Arepas, if you have successfully eliminated all cracks, steam will build up inside and they will puff and swell. It takes some practice, but it's well worth the effort.

4. When the oil is ready, place each portion of dough carefully in the pan, and fry until golden brown, turning over once during frying and frying for 4 to 5 minutes per side. Do not crowd the pan. Fry in batches.

5. Drain Arepas on towels before serving. With a wet serrated knife, slice the Arepas in half horizontally and serve warm or at room temperature.

Crispy Asian-Style Tofu

MAKES 4 SERVINGS

I often bake tofu by simply tossing it with kosher salt, freshly ground black pepper, and olive oil and then baking it in a single layer in a 400°F oven for about 15 minutes, or until the edges begin to brown. Then I pair it with fried rice and broccoli crowns, and dinner is served. When that starts to become humdrum, I go the extra mile and soak the tofu in an Asian-style marinade before baking it, as in this recipe.

½ cup gluten-free soy sauce (I like La Choy Lite)

6 tablespoons rice vinegar

¼ cup honey

¼ cup sesame (or vegetable) oil

1 cup **Vegetable Stock** (see page 131)

1 tablespoon fresh ginger, minced

1 (14-ounce) block extra-firm tofu

2 tablespoons cornstarch

1. Make the sauce first, because you will dry the tofu and then soak it in the sauce. In a medium-size saucepan, place the soy sauce, vinegar, honey, oil, Vegetable Stock, and ginger and whisk well to combine. Over medium-high heat, bring the sauce to a boil. Lower the heat and, stirring constantly, allow the sauce to simmer until it has begun to reduce and thicken. Remove the sauce from the heat, transfer it to a medium-size flat bowl, and allow it cool for at least 10 minutes.

2. Remove the tofu from its package, drain it, and wrap it in a clean kitchen towel. Gently but firmly squeeze the tofu in the towel to drain it of as much water as possible. Remove the tofu from the towel and slice it into cubes about ¾ inch square. Place the cubes into the bowl with the cooled sauce, and allow them to marinate at room temperature for at least 45 minutes to an hour. If the cubes are not covered completely by the sauce, turn them a few times while they marinate.

3. Preheat your oven to 350°F. Line a large, rimmed baking sheet with aluminum foil and spray it with nonstick cooking spray. Once the tofu has finished marinating, with tongs or clean fingers, carefully remove each piece of tofu from the marinade and place all of them on the prepared baking sheet in neat rows, about ¼ inch apart. Do not discard the marinade. Place the baking sheet in the center of the preheated oven and bake until crisped, about 15 to 17 minutes. The tofu may blacken a bit, since the sugar in the honey will caramelize, but take care not to allow it to burn.

4. While the tofu is baking, return the marinade to the saucepan, add 2 tablespoons of cornstarch, and whisk to combine well. Return the saucepan to the stove top and heat it over medium heat until the sauce thickens again, whisking constantly.

5. Serve the tofu over brown rice. Top with the sauce.

Tomato Soup

MAKES ABOUT 6 CUPS

With its deep red color and luxurious thickness, this tomato soup is more versatile and robust than you might otherwise imagine. It is deliciously simple served with a buttered **Dinner Roll** (page 98) or some **Cheese Crackers** (page 58), but it can also be a warm and filling meal when served with rice and beans.

1 (28-ounce) can whole, peeled tomatoes (preferably with basil)

1½ teaspoons kosher salt

Freshly ground black pepper, to taste

4 tablespoons extra-virgin olive oil

1 medium yellow onion, diced

3 cloves garlic, crushed whole and peeled

2 tablespoons dried oregano

2 tablespoons tomato paste

2 carrots, peeled and finely diced

2 large roasting potatoes, peeled and medium diced

2 cups **Vegetable Stock** (see page 131)

2 cups water

1. Preheat your oven to 375°F. Line a rimmed baking sheet with aluminum foil and grease with cooking spray. Remove the tomatoes from the can, drain them (reserving the liquid), ensure that all the tomatoes are well peeled, slice them in half, and place them in a single layer on the prepared baking sheet. Sprinkle the tomatoes with ½ teaspoon of the salt and pepper to taste, then drizzle them evenly with 2 tablespoons olive oil. Place the baking sheet in the center of the preheated oven and bake until the tomatoes begin to brown, about 20 to 25 minutes.

2. While the tomatoes are roasting, in a medium-size saucepan, heat the remaining 2 tablespoons of oil over medium-high heat. Add the onions and crushed whole garlic and cook until the onions are translucent and the garlic fragrant, 4 to 5 minutes. Crush the dried oregano between your palms to release

the herb's oils before adding the oregano and the tomato paste to the saucepan. Stir to combine. Add the carrots, potatoes, Vegetable Stock, and water and continue to cook until the liquid is boiling. Turn the heat down to a simmer and cook until the carrots and potatoes are beginning to soften, about 10 minutes.

3. Add the roasted tomatoes and all of the roasting bits from the baking sheet to the saucepan, stir to combine, and return the soup to a simmer. Allow the soup to simmer gently, uncovered, until it thickens and the carrots and potatoes are very tender, about another 15 to 20 minutes.

4. For a smoother consistency, puree a portion of the soup with an immersion blender.

Shoestring Savings

Tomato Soup

On a shoestring: $4.85 for 6 cups

If you bought it: $10.26 for 6 cups (canned)

Noodle Kugel

MAKES 6 TO 8 SERVINGS

I wish I had a better name for this, but "noodle pudding" doesn't quite fit, so we'll stick with Noodle Kugel. It's a decadent blend of noodles, eggs, butter, cream cheese, sour cream, and ricotta cheese, baked with a cereal topping. I suspect it's a dessert masquerading as food, so there are more than a few cheers when I treat my children to it.

1 pound short, gluten-free dried pasta (like penne, spirals, or small shells)

1 stick (8 tablespoons) unsalted butter

8 extra-large eggs, separated

½ cup plus 2 tablespoons confectioner's sugar

1 (8-ounce) package cream cheese, at room temperature

1½ cups sour cream (low-fat is fine, nonfat is not)

1 pound (16 ounces) ricotta or cottage cheese (a nondairy substitute will not work here)

¼ teaspoon kosher salt

⅛ teaspoon cream of tartar

TOPPING

4 tablespoons unsalted butter, melted

⅔ cup crushed gluten-free corn flakes

1. Preheat your oven to 350°F. Grease a 9 x 13-inch baking dish with unsalted butter and set it aside.

2. In a large pot of boiling water, cook the pasta to an al dente texture, drain it, and return it to the hot pot. To the pasta, add the 8 tablespoons of butter, and stir to melt the butter and coat the pasta. Set the pot aside.

3. In a separate large bowl, cream the egg yolks, sugar, cream cheese, sour cream, ricotta cheese, and the salt, beating until pale golden in color. Beat the egg whites with the cream of tartar in another separate bowl until stiff peaks form and then carefully fold the egg whites into the egg yolk mixture with a wide spatula. Add the mixture to the pasta pot, and stir gently with the wide

spatula to combine well, then scrape everything into the prepared baking dish, smoothing the top.

4. In a small bowl, combine the melted butter and crushed corn flakes and mix well. Sprinkle the topping over the pasta mixture in the baking dish as evenly as possible. Cover the baking dish completely with aluminum foil and place it in the center of the preheated oven and bake for 45 minutes. Then uncover the dish and bake for another 10 to 15 minutes, or until lightly browned on top.

5. Cut the kugel into squares and serve warm or at room temperature.

Sweet and Sour Beets

MAKES ABOUT 4 CUPS OF SLICED BEETS

Beets are so costly to buy already prepared and terribly easy to prepare on your own. Chopped, they make a lovely addition to any salad and pair beautifully with a salty cheese, like feta. And this sweet and sour marinade is great for pickling tomatoes, cucumbers, and even hard-boiled eggs. But, remember: you don't pickle pickles—they're already pickled.

3–4 medium-size raw beets
½ cup apple cider vinegar
½ cup sugar
⅛ teaspoon kosher salt
¼ teaspoon ground cinnamon

1. Preheat your oven to 375°F. Do not wash the beets, since that will cause them to steam when you put them in the oven. You want them to bake dry. Trim the greens ½ inch from the top of each beet and clean them with a dry paper towel. Wrap each beet separately and tightly in aluminum foil. Place the beets in the preheated oven and bake for 60 to 75 minutes, or until they are still firm but can be pierced easily with a fork.

2. Remove the beets from the oven and allow them to cool until you are able to handle them. Unwrap each beet and peel the skin off. It should come off easily. If you are particularly concerned about staining your fingers, use rubber gloves. The stain will come off readily if you wash your hands promptly after handling the beets. Slice the beets about ⅛ inch to ¼ inch thick, and set them aside.

3. In a medium-size saucepan, place the vinegar, sugar, salt, and cinnamon and stir to combine. Bring the mixture to a simmer over medium-high heat, stirring occasionally to ensure that the sugar dissolves in the vinegar. Gently place the sliced beets in the saucepan, return to a simmer and cook, uncovered, for about 5 minutes.

4. Place the beets and all of the liquid into an airtight container. They will marinate and only get better over time. If you are so inclined, you may can them.

Glazed Carrots

MAKES 4 TO 5 SIDE-DISH SERVINGS

To make quick work of this recipe, complete the first step, blanching the carrots, one day ahead. These carrots are a bit sweet, but balanced nicely with just enough acidity that you know it's still dinner, not dessert. Serve it at Thanksgiving or any old time. Hey, better this than candied yams.

2 pounds carrots, peeled and cut on the diagonal into ½-inch pieces
2 tablespoons canola oil
1 cup **Vegetable Stock** (see page 131)
8 tablespoons (½ cup) honey
2 tablespoons balsamic vinegar
¼ teaspoon kosher salt
Freshly ground black pepper, to taste
2 tablespoons unsalted butter

1. Blanch the carrots by placing them in a medium-size pot of boiling water for 2 minutes. Remove carrots from the boiling water and place them in a bath of ice and water for 2 minutes. Then drain them of all water with a sieve, or simply remove them from the ice bath with a slotted spoon and blot them with a towel. If you decide to make this recipe in stages, stop here and store the blanched carrots in an airtight container overnight in the refrigerator. Pick up with the next step the following day.

2. In a large skillet, cook the carrots in the oil over medium-high heat for 2 minutes, until they begin to brown. Add the stock, honey, vinegar, salt, pepper, and butter to the skillet and mix to combine. Bring the mixture to a boil, then reduce the heat and allow the mixture to simmer, stirring occasionally, until the sauce is thickened, about 5 to 6 minutes. Serve warm or at room temperature.

Cornmeal Spoonbread

MAKES 4 SERVINGS

This spoonbread is something like a soufflé, but I don't separate the eggs. I used to separate the eggs, whip up the whites with terrific effort, then gently fold them in. The dish was beautifully domed and fell a bit within 5 minutes of being taken out of the oven. Then one day, just like that, I stopped separating the eggs. If there was a difference in how puffy the final product was after 5 minutes of taking the dish out of the oven, I'll be a monkey's uncle. If you ever have occasion to make gluten-free cornmeal spoonbread for the Queen of England, go the extra mile and separate the eggs.

2 cups milk (low-fat is fine, nonfat is not)
4 tablespoons unsalted butter
½ teaspoon kosher salt
1 cup yellow cornmeal
4 extra-large eggs, lightly beaten

1. Preheat the oven to 375°F. Grease a 6-inch diameter ovenproof casserole dish with unsalted butter and set it aside.

2. In a medium saucepan, slowly heat the milk, butter, and salt until the mixture boils. Once it boils, turn down to a simmer, add the cornmeal, and cook, whisking constantly. It will suddenly come together. Set the mixture aside to cool for about 10 minutes.

3. Once the mixture has cooled, add the eggs, one at a time, whisking well after each addition, until smooth. Spoon the mixture into the prepared casserole dish, place it in the middle of the preheated oven, and bake for 1 hour, until browned on top.

4. Cut two small slits into the top of the spoonbread as soon as it comes out of the oven. This will allow some steam to escape and the casserole to remain puffy. Serve immediately.

Berry Scones, page 82

Popovers, page 122

Brioche Bread, page 108

Tomato Soup, page 140,
with **Cheese Crackers,** page 58

Chicken and Dumplings,
page 170

White Sandwich Bread,

page 104

Spinach Pie, page 134

Pizza Dough, page 44

Chocolate Sandwich Cookies,
page 205

Chocolate Chip Cookies,
page 200

Tomato Polenta

MAKES 4 SERVINGS

This is similar to the basic polenta we make for **Polenta Pizza** (page 130), but it's jazzed up with tomatoes. Since the tomatoes add a bunch of moisture to the mixture, we use as much cornmeal as we do milk to keep everything in proper balance. This dish is warm and comforting and makes a beautiful base for some grilled chicken.

1 (28-ounce) can whole, peeled tomatoes

1 cup milk (low-fat is fine, nonfat is not)

1 teaspoon kosher salt

1 cup yellow cornmeal

½ cup grated Parmesan cheese (plus more for topping)

1. Remove the tomatoes from the can, chop them roughly, and set them aside. In a large saucepan, warm the milk over medium heat until simmering gently. You don't want it to boil. Add the chopped tomatoes with their juice, plus the salt, to the pan and stir to combine. The acid in the tomatoes may cause the milk to begin to curdle, which is fine.

2. Continue to heat the milk mixture until it returns to simmering. Once the liquid is simmering, add the cornmeal in a slow but steady stream, whisking constantly, making sure there are no lumps. Reduce the heat to low, and continue to whisk until the mixture thickens, about 5 to 7 minutes. Remove the pan from the heat and stir in the Parmesan cheese until it is fully incorporated and melted. Serve with a few extra shavings of Parmesan cheese.

Seven

Comforting Dinners: Just Like "Mom" Used to Make

Macaroni & Cheese

MAKES 4 SERVINGS

This recipe for macaroni and cheese can be made on the stove top and eaten as is or poured into a 9 x 13-inch baking dish, covered, and baked until firm. Only one of my children will eat the stove top version, and I have to assume it's a matter of texture. All three of them will eat it baked. This is also a great make-ahead dish. Just cook it on the stove top, pour it into a prepared baking dish, cover it tightly with plastic wrap and foil, and freeze it. When you are ready to serve it, there is no need to defrost it first. Just remove the plastic wrap but retain the foil, pop it in a preheated oven, and bake according to the recipe directions.

1 pound (16 ounces) short gluten-free pasta (elbows, penne, small shells, etc.)

1 stick (8 tablespoons) unsalted butter

4 extra-large eggs

1 can (12 ounces) evaporated milk

1 teaspoon kosher salt

Freshly ground black pepper, to taste

3 cups grated cheddar or mozzarella cheese (or a combination)

1. In a large pot of boiling water, cook the pasta to an al dente texture (shave a couple of minutes off the package directions). Drain the pasta and return it to the hot pot, off the stove top.

2. Add the butter to the pot of cooked pasta and toss gently until the butter is entirely melted into the hot pasta. It should only take you 2 minutes or less.

3. Beat the eggs in a separate, medium bowl. Add the milk, salt, and pepper to the eggs and whisk to combine. Add a few tablespoons of the hot pasta to the egg mixture. This will temper the eggs by slowly coaxing them up to a warmer temperature. This is how we'll avoid scrambling the eggs.

4. Add the egg mixture to the pasta pot, then the grated cheese, and stir gently to combine without breaking the pasta into unrecognizable pieces. If you're making Baked Macaroni & Cheese, preheat your oven to 375°F, and grease a 9 x 13-inch baking dish with unsalted butter.

5. Return the pot to the stove top and cook over a very low flame, folding over the mixture gently. Continue cooking for about 2 to 3 minutes, until the mixture is creamy and the cheese is melted. If you're making Stove Top Macaroni & Cheese, your job is done. If not, carry on to the next step.

6. For the baked variety, spread the entire mixture evenly into a greased 9 x 13-inch baking dish, cover the dish with foil, and bake in the preheated oven for 40 minutes or until it is bubbling around the edges and the eggs are set. Uncover and bake for another 7 to 10 minutes until browned on top. Cool 10 minutes, then slice into squares and serve.

Shoestring Savings

Macaroni & Cheese

On a shoestring: $7.36 for 4 servings

If you bought it: $17.96 for 4 servings (frozen)

Szechuan Meatballs

The secret to flavorful Szechuan meatballs is to allow the ground beef to marinate so it absorbs all the flavors in the soy sauce, honey, vinegar, and ginger. Be sure to use ground beef that is at least 90 percent lean. If you use beef that is less lean, the fat drains onto the pan when the meatballs are baked, and much of the flavor drains right along with it. Pity. The sesame oil in the marinade is much tastier and less greasy than the fat in the ground beef. I usually serve these meatballs with **Lo Mein** (page 154) and **Hoisin Sauce** (page 54).

¼ cup gluten-free soy sauce (I like La Choy Lite)

2 tablespoons honey

⅛ teaspoon freshly ground black pepper

¼ cup rice vinegar

4 tablespoons sesame oil

2 tablespoons fresh ginger, minced

2 tablespoons cornstarch

2 extra-large eggs, beaten

1½ teaspoons **Chinese-Style Hot Sauce** (optional) (page 52)

1½ pounds (at least 90 percent lean) ground beef

1. Preheat the oven to 375°F.

2. In a large bowl, whisk together the soy sauce, honey, pepper, vinegar, sesame oil, ginger, cornstarch, eggs, and (optional) hot sauce, until well combined.

3. Add the ground beef to the bowl. With clean hands (or a large fork), mix to combine the sauce with the ground beef. After mixing, allow the beef to absorb the other ingredients by covering the bowl and letting it sit at room temperature for 10 to 15 minutes.

4. Divide the meat mixture into balls, each 1½ inches in diameter. Arrange 1 inch apart on lined rimmed baking sheets.

5. Bake in the preheated oven for 20 to 25 minutes, or until nicely browned.

Apple-Leek-Sausage Corn Bread Stuffing Dinner

MAKES 6 SERVINGS

I had always made this corn bread stuffing with apples and leeks, but it's so hearty and everyone in my family loves it so well that I started experimenting with adding some protein to make it a satisfying main dish. The sausage, removed from its casing and crumbled, does just the trick. And the old-fashioned corn bread helps to stretch the sausage, so it feeds more hungry people.

1½ pounds sweet sausage, casing removed

6 tablespoons unsalted butter

3 leeks, trimmed and sliced thinly in cross-section

5 McIntosh apples, peeled, cored, and diced

2 tablespoons poultry seasoning

Kosher salt and freshly ground black pepper, to taste

3 tablespoons fresh parsley, chopped

1 recipe **Old-Fashioned Gluten-Free Corn Bread** (page 80), crumbled

3 extra-large eggs, beaten

¼ cup milk (low-fat is fine, nonfat is not)

2 cups **Chicken Stock** (page 35)

1. In a medium saucepan over a medium flame, heat the sausage until cooked through and browned. It helps to break up the sausage into small pieces while it is cooking. The sausage cooks faster, and you can then better distribute it throughout the stuffing. Remove the sausage from the pan and set it aside to drain in a medium-size bowl.

2. In the same medium saucepan with the sausage drippings, melt the butter over very low heat. Once the butter is melted, add the leeks, apples, poultry seasoning, salt and pepper, and parsley and cook, covered, over medium-low heat until the leeks and apples are soft and the flavors married. The mixture should be very fragrant.

3. Add the crumbled corn bread to the mixture and stir to combine. Break up any very large pieces with your stirring spoon. Set aside the mixture to cool for about 10 to 15 minutes.

4. Preheat the oven to 375°F. Grease a 9 x 12-inch dish with unsalted butter and set it aside.

5. Combine the eggs and milk in a separate small bowl and whisk to combine. Then add the chicken stock and mix to combine. After the stuffing mixture has cooled off, temper the beaten egg mixture by adding a few spoonfuls of the stuffing mixture and stirring gently. This allows the eggs to get accustomed to the temperature of the warm stuffing mixture without being scrambled. Add the tempered egg mixture to the rest of the stuffing mixture and stir gently until combined. Add the sausage to the mixture and stir until the sausage is evenly distributed throughout.

6. Spread the mixture evenly in the greased baking dish and smooth the top. You don't want any big pieces of corn bread sticking up. They'll burn when you brown the stuffing.

7. Cover the dish completely with foil and place it in the preheated oven. Bake for 35 to 40 minutes or until the egg is set. Uncover and bake for another 7 to 10 minutes, until the stuffing is nicely browned. Serve warm or at room temperature.

Lo Mein

MAKES 4 TO 5 SERVINGS

There are a few Chinese restaurants near my home that serve gluten-free food. Although it's wonderful to have as an option, and I'm appreciative, we almost never go. When we're craving Chinese food, I usually would just rather make my own. With the money we'd spend on going to a restaurant, I can make dinner and dessert for a few nights straight. This recipe has just the right balance of spices and sweetness. I usually serve it with **Szechuan Meatballs** (page 151) and **Hoisin Sauce** (page 54).

2 cloves garlic, minced

2 tablespoons sesame oil

3½ cups **Chicken Stock** (page 35)

½ teaspoon freshly ground black pepper

2 tablespoons honey

2 tablespoons brown sugar

2 tablespoons molasses

2 tablespoons rice vinegar

½ cup gluten-free soy sauce (I like La Choy Lite)

2 tablespoons cornstarch

1 pound (16-ounces) gluten-free spaghetti

Shoestring Savings

Lo Mein

On a shoestring: $6.90 for 4 to 5 servings

If you bought it: $20.00 for 4 to 5 servings

(frozen)

1. In a medium saucepan, sauté the garlic in sesame oil until fragrant (about 2 to 3 minutes). Add the Chicken Stock, pepper, honey, brown sugar, molasses, vinegar, soy sauce, and cornstarch to the saucepan. Whisk until the ingredients are well combined. Bring to a boil, then lower the heat to medium-high and simmer gently for about 20 minutes, or until the mixture is reduced by nearly half and is thickened.

2. While the sauce is reducing, boil a large pot of water. To the boiling water, add the spaghetti and cook to al dente. Drain the spaghetti, rinse it with cold water, drain it again, and place it in a large serving bowl. Pour the thickened sauce over the spaghetti and toss it with tongs to coat.

Beef "Pot Pie"

MAKES 6 SERVINGS

This dish is similar to beef lasagna, but since the pasta starts out dry and boils in Chicken Stock in the oven, it's richer and more satisfying (and significantly less time consuming to make). Add some bite-size broccoli crowns to the sour cream and ricotta mixture, and you have a complete meal.

1 medium onion, chopped

2 tablespoons extra-virgin olive oil

2 cloves garlic, minced

1½ pounds lean ground beef

¼ teaspoon kosher salt

Freshly ground black pepper, to taste

3 cups tomato sauce

8 ounces sour cream (low-fat is fine, nonfat is not)

8 ounces part skim ricotta cheese

1 pound (16 ounces) short gluten-free pasta (elbows, penne, small shells, etc.)

2 cups **Chicken Stock** (page 35)

1½ cups grated mozzarella cheese

1 recipe **Pizza Dough** (page 44), chilled

1. Preheat the oven to 375°F. Grease a 9 x 13-inch baking dish with unsalted butter and set it aside.

2. In a medium skillet, over medium-high heat, sauté the chopped onion in the oil until the onion is translucent, about 5 minutes. Add the garlic to the pan and sauté until fragrant, about 2 minutes. Add the ground beef and cook until the beef is browned and cooked all the way through. Season with salt and pepper. Add 1½ cups of the tomato sauce to the beef mixture, stir to combine, and set the mixture aside.

3. In a medium-size bowl, combine the sour cream and ricotta cheese until well blended.

4. Spoon the remaining 1½ cups of tomato sauce evenly over the bottom of the prepared baking dish. Sprinkle the dry pasta over the top of the tomato sauce, then pour the 2 cups of Chicken Stock over the pasta. The pasta will absorb much of the liquid. Spread the sour cream and ricotta cheese mixture, then top with the beef mixture, each in a single layer across the pan. Sprinkle the mozzarella cheese evenly across the top.

5. Cover the baking dish with foil and bake in the preheated oven for 30 to 35 minutes. While the dish is in the oven, roll the pizza dough between two sheets of plastic wrap into a 12 x 15-inch rectangle.

6. After the first 30 to 35 minutes of baking, remove the baking dish from the oven and remove the foil. Place the pizza dough on top of the baking dish, and carefully secure around the edges (the dish will be quite hot). Return the dish to the oven and bake 7 to 10 minutes more, until the dough is lightly browned on top. Allow to cool at least 15 minutes before serving.

Chicken Pot Pie

MAKES 4 SERVINGS

Traditional chicken pot pies like this one are simple to make but somehow make a dramatic presentation for guests when you divide the recipe into personal-size pies. They smell like heaven, and taste even better, especially when you get a perfect spoonful with just the right balance of buttery, flaky pastry crust and creamy, warm, and satisfying chicken and vegetable filling. And they can be assembled completely, then frozen for up to a month before baking.

½ recipe **Savory Pastry Crust**, chilled (page 41)

3 large yellow onions, chopped

3 tablespoons extra-virgin olive oil

1 stick (8 tablespoons) unsalted butter

½ cup all-purpose gluten-free flour

¼ teaspoon xanthan gum

4 to 6 cups **Chicken Stock** (page 35)

¼ cup milk (low-fat is fine, nonfat is not)

¼ teaspoon kosher salt

⅛ teaspoon freshly ground black pepper

3–4 carrots, skinned, chopped, and blanched

1 (10-ounce) package frozen peas

5–6 skin-on, bone-in split chicken breasts, roasted, cooled, and cubed

1 extra-large egg beaten with 1 tablespoon water (for egg wash)

1. Preheat the oven to 375°F. Grease a round ovenproof baking dish, at least 10 inches in diameter, with unsalted butter. Set the dish aside.

2. Place the pastry crust dough between two sheets of plastic wrap, shape into a disk, and roll out the dough until it is about ⅛ inch thick. Place the rolled-out dough, still flat between the two sheets of plastic wrap, in the refrigerator to chill.

3. In the meantime, make the filling. In a large saucepan, sauté the onions over medium-high heat in the oil and butter until the onions are translucent but

not browned, 7 to 10 minutes. Reduce the heat to low and add the flour and xanthan gum, stirring constantly, until the flour is well incorporated and the mixture begins to smell a bit nutty, 2 to 3 minutes. Add the Chicken Stock, milk, salt, and pepper and stir to combine. Raise the heat to medium-high once again and cook until the mixture simmers.

4. Once the mixture is simmering, add the blanched carrots and frozen peas. Stir the mixture until all the ingredients are well combined. Pour the filling into the prepared baking dish. If making personal pot pies, divide the filling between 4 oven-safe baking dishes, approximately 6 inches in diameter each.

5. Remove the pastry dough from the refrigerator and gently peel and replace the plastic wrap from one side of the dough. Turn the dough over, and gently peel the plastic wrap from the other side of the dough. Place the dough, uncovered side down, on top of the baking dish. Gently remove the other sheet of plastic wrap from the top of the pie. Crimp the dough all around the perimeter of the pie, pressing it together with your fingers to seal it. With a very sharp knife, carefully cut an "X" in the middle of the pie to allow steam to escape during baking. With a pastry brush, paint the top of the pie with the egg wash. Again, if you are making four separate personal pot pies, divide the dough evenly among the tops of the baking dishes in a similar manner to that described above.

6. Place the baking dish (or the 4 individual dishes) on a rimmed baking sheet, and place in the preheated oven and bake for about 1 hour, until the top is lightly golden.

Chicken en Croute

MAKES 4 SERVINGS

I don't make Chicken en Croute too often, because I fear that afterward my children will refuse all chicken served without cheese and preserves and cloaked in pastry. It's kind of like sleeping in a tent in the desert, and thinking it's a fine life, until you sleep on clean, fresh sheets. You can't go back. Try this mix of sweet and savory, wrapped in flaky and buttery pastry, and I doubt you'll go back, either.

1½ pounds boneless, skinless chicken breast

Kosher salt and freshly ground black pepper, to taste

¼ cup fresh parsley, chopped (or 2 tablespoons dried parsley)

2 tablespoons extra-virgin olive oil

1 recipe **Savory Pastry Dough** (page 41), chilled in the refrigerator for at least an hour

4 ounces grated mozzarella cheese

½ cup apricot preserves

1 extra-large egg, beaten with 1 tablespoon water (for egg wash)

1. Slice the chicken into a large dice, with pieces about 1 inch square, and season it with salt, pepper, and parsley. In a medium-size skillet, heat the oil over medium-high heat. Brown the chicken on both sides, about 4 minutes total. Remove the chicken from the heat and set it aside.

2. Remove the pastry dough from the refrigerator and pull it into two parts, handling as little as possible. Cover each portion of dough in two pieces of plastic wrap and roll each to ⅛ inch thickness. Refrigerate the dough again for another 10 to 15 minutes, then take it out and remove the plastic wrap. If the dough is sticky at all, dust with a bit of flour on both sides. Slice the dough into rectangles, approximately 3 x 6 inches.

3. Preheat your oven to 400°F. Line baking sheets with parchment paper and set them aside.

4. Shred some chicken and place some on one side of each rectangle of dough, then top with cheese and a spoonful of preserves. Fold over and pinch to secure the edges.

5. Transfer the pastries to the prepared baking sheets. Brush the egg wash over the top and seams of each pastry. This will help keep the pastries from opening and help them brown in the oven.

6. Place the baking sheets into the center of the preheated oven and bake for 12 to 15 minutes, or until golden. Serve warm or at room temperature.

Meatlove

MAKES ENOUGH MEATBALLS OR MEATLOAF TO SERVE 6 PEOPLE

If there is a truly meaningful difference between meatloaf and meatballs in the home kitchen, it has thus far eluded me. I use one basic recipe for both shapes of this flavorful mixture of ground beef, breadcrumbs, cheese, eggs, milk, and spices, and we call it Meatlove, since that is what my son thought it was called when he was rather small, and the name stuck. Who wants to eat something called "meatloaf" anyhow? It's descriptive, sure, but not exactly appetizing. Meatlove it is, then. And love it, we do.

1 cup milk (low-fat is fine, nonfat is not)

2 to 3 slices stale gluten-free bread, crumbled (you can substitute about 1 cup prepared gluten-free breadcrumbs, and then reduce the milk to ½ cup)

4 extra-large eggs, beaten

½ cup grated mozzarella cheese

¼ cup grated Parmesan cheese

2 tablespoons dried oregano (or 1 tablespoon chopped fresh oregano)

1 tablespoon dried basil (or 1½ teaspoons roughly chopped fresh basil)

1 tablespoon dried parsley (or 1½ teaspoons chopped fresh flat-leaf parsley)

2 cloves garlic, minced

Kosher salt and freshly ground black pepper, to taste

2 pounds ground beef

2 to 4 cups tomato sauce (optional)

¼ to ½ cup extra-virgin olive oil (optional)

1. In a medium bowl, combine the milk and bread (if you are using prepared breadcrumbs, skip this step). Set the bowl aside and allow the bread to soak in the milk for about 10 minutes, until the bread has softened and absorbed at least half the milk.

2. In a large bowl, place the eggs, cheeses, oregano, basil, parsley, garlic, salt, and pepper and beat to combine well. When the bread is finished soaking, remove it from the milk, add it to the large bowl with the other ingredients, and

stir to combine (if you are using prepared breadcrumbs, add the milk and the prepared breadcrumbs to the large bowl, and stir to combine). Discard the rest of the milk. Add the meat to the large bowl, and, with clean hands, mix all the ingredients together thoroughly.

3. **If you are making meatballs:** Grease an oven-safe dish with at least 2-inch high sides and preheat your oven to 350°F. Divide the beef mixture into portions and shape into round meatballs about 1 inch in diameter. Place the meatballs at least 1 inch apart from one another in the baking dish, cover with tomato sauce or drizzle with olive oil, and place in the center of the preheated oven and bake for approximately 35 minutes, until cooked through.

4. **If you are making meatloaf (or "Meatlove"):** Line a rimmed baking sheet with parchment paper, and preheat your oven to 350°F. Place the beef mixture onto the prepared baking sheet and shape into a loaf, place in the center of the oven and bake for 45 to 60 minutes, until cooked through. If the top begins to brown before the meatloaf is cooked all the way through, tent it with a piece of foil. Slice about ½ to ¾ inch thick to serve.

Shepherd's Pie

MAKES 4 TO 6 SERVINGS

Shepherd's Pie is one of those classic comfort foods that never disappoints. The essential elements are the browned ground beef, some vegetable, spices, and a mashed potato topping, so feel free to play with the types of vegetables and the types of potatoes that you use. I always use zucchini, since it is so tasty with tomato sauce and adds nice moisture, and I prefer a mixture of red skin and sweet potatoes to make a colorful and savory crust. If you're feeling very generous, instead of the mashed potato crust, top the pie with rounds of raw **Sweet Potato Biscuits** (page 102), and bake as usual, or until the biscuits are nicely browned.

2 tablespoons extra-virgin olive oil

1 large onion, chopped

1 to 2 large carrots, peeled and chopped

1 large zucchini, chopped

1 pound lean ground beef

1 cup **Chicken Stock** (page 35)

3 tablespoons tomato paste

2 tablespoons Worcestershire sauce

3 tablespoons chopped fresh parsley (or 1½ tablespoons dried)

1–2 tablespoons all-purpose gluten-free flour

2 pounds potatoes (a mixture of red skin and sweet potatoes, or either one alone), peeled

3 tablespoons unsalted butter

½ cup milk (low-fat is fine, nonfat is not)

Kosher salt, to taste

1. Preheat your oven to 375°F. Grease a 4-quart baking dish with unsalted butter and set it aside.

2. In a large pan, heat the oil over medium-high heat. Add the onion, zucchini, and carrot and cook until all the vegetables are soft and the onion and zucchini are translucent, about 7 minutes. Add the ground beef and cook until

browned, another 5 minutes. If you are using fatty beef, drain and discard at least half the fat. Add the Chicken Stock, tomato paste, Worcestershire sauce, parsley, and flour and simmer uncovered until the mixture thickens, about 10 minutes. Spoon the beef mixture into the prepared baking dish, and set it aside.

3. In a medium to large pot, boil the potatoes in salted water, then reduce to a simmer and cook partly covered until the potatoes are fork tender, about 20 minutes. Drain the water from the potatoes and mash them. Add the butter and milk to the potatoes and salt to taste. Spread the mashed potatoes over the beef mixture. Make a crosshatch pattern over the top with a fork.

4. Bake in the center of the preheated oven for about 30 minutes. Move the dish up to the top of the oven and turn on the broiler for the last few minutes to crisp the potato crust.

Shoestring Savings

Shepherd's Pie

On a shoestring: $1.26 per serving

If you bought it: $5.00 per serving (frozen)

Beef Potstickers

MAKES 4 SERVINGS

I won't lie to you: I don't fry these. I am sure they would be delicious fried, but they're just enough work as it is. To me, eating them as is strikes the right balance between effort and enjoyment. If you're craving fried potstickers, though, shallow fry these after they're boiled. And then be a good friend and send some to me.

¼ cup gluten-free soy sauce (I like La Choy Lite)
1 tablespoon honey
⅛ teaspoon freshly ground black pepper
4 tablespoons rice vinegar
2 tablespoons fresh ginger, minced
2 tablespoons cornstarch
1½ pounds lean ground beef
15 to 20 **Wonton Wrappers** (page 48)

1. In a large bowl, whisk together the soy sauce, honey, pepper, rice vinegar, ginger, and cornstarch until well combined.

2. Add the ground beef to the bowl. With clean hands (or a large fork), mix to combine the sauce with the ground beef. After mixing, allow the beef to absorb the other ingredients by covering the bowl and letting it sit at room temperature for 10 to 15 minutes.

3. With wet hands, pinch off a portion of the ground beef that is approximately ¾ inch in diameter and place it in the center of one Wonton Wrapper, leaving a border of at least 1 inch all around the wrapper. Again with wet hands, moisten the border of the Wonton Wrapper and fold it over, then press the edges together to seal it closed. Repeat the process with the remaining Wonton Wrappers.

4. Heat a large pot of boiling water, salt it liberally as it begins to boil, and gently drop the dumplings in the boiling water one at a time, in batches so the pot is never too crowded, until cooked through, about 5 to 7 minutes. Remove the dumplings from the water carefully and serve hot or warm, with **Hoisin Sauce** (page 54).

Lemon Chicken, Chinese Style

MAKES 4 SERVINGS

You do not need a wok to make this dish. It's nice to use a wok, since the food cooks a bit quicker and a wok requires less oil than shallow frying, but at the end of the day, it's unnecessary. This really does taste authentic, and frying the chicken in small pieces like this and serving it over rice helps stretch the chicken, while leaving your dinner guests satisfied and content.

⅔ cup **Chicken Stock** (page 35)

Zest and juice of 2 lemons

4 tablespoons gluten-free soy sauce (I like La Choy Lite)

1 tablespoon light brown sugar

2 extra-large eggs

½ cup cornstarch (or more, as needed)

1 pound boneless, skinless chicken breast, cut into small pieces (or strips)

½ cup canola oil

3 to 4 cloves garlic, minced

2 teaspoons ginger, minced (optional)

1. In a medium bowl, whisk together the Chicken Stock, lemon zest, lemon juice, soy sauce, and brown sugar. Set it aside.

2. In a large bowl, beat the eggs with a couple tablespoons of water. Place cornstarch in a shallow dish. Dredge the chicken through the egg wash, allowing any excess to drop off, then place in the cornstarch to coat lightly, shaking off any excess.

3. In a wok (or a large sauté pan, with more oil, to shallow fry), heat the oil over medium-high heat. Add the chicken and fry until crisp, 2 to 3 minutes total, turning once. Remove the chicken and drain on paper towels. Repeat in batches if necessary, and add more oil as needed.

4. Add the soy sauce mixture to the pan with the garlic (and the optional ginger) and bring to a boil. Return the chicken to the pan and stir fry to warm, turning over to coat with the sauce. Serve over rice.

Tortilla Soup

MAKES 4 SERVINGS

I love taking a basic dish like chicken soup and classing it up a bit. I find that it's a good way to keep the dinner doldrums at bay and also to gently diversify my children's palates. The first time I served them tortilla soup, I went light on the jalapeños, removing the seeds and the ribs, and mincing the peppers very fine.

2 medium yellow onions (or 1 large), chopped

2 tablespoons extra-virgin olive oil

2 cloves of garlic, minced

2 jalapeños, seeded and minced (remove the ribs, too, for less heat)

1 (28-ounce) can whole, peeled tomatoes, cut into chunks

3 tablespoons tomato paste

1 quart (4 cups) **Chicken Stock** (page 35)

½ teaspoon kosher salt

Freshly ground black pepper, to taste

1 teaspoon ground cumin

2–3 tablespoons canola oil

8 corn tortillas, cut into strips ⅛ inch wide

1½ cups shredded, cooked chicken

1. In a large saucepan, sauté the onions in oil over medium-high heat until translucent, about 5 minutes. Add the garlic and sauté until fragrant, about 2 minutes.

2. Add the jalapeños, tomatoes, tomato paste, Chicken Stock, salt, pepper, and cumin. Simmer over medium heat, stirring occasionally, until thickened, about 15 minutes.

3. Preheat the oven to 400°F. Grease a rimmed baking sheet with unsalted butter (or line with parchment paper) and spread the strips of corn tortilla on the sheet. Toss the strips with the oil, salt, and pepper to taste. Place the baking

sheet in the oven and bake until browned, about 10 minutes, shaking the pan after 5 minutes.

4. Serve by ladling the soup into bowls, topping with about a half cup of shredded cooked chicken and a handful of tortilla strips. Serve immediately.

Chicken and Dumplings

MAKES 6 SERVINGS

I almost always have a quart or two of this thick, homey chicken soup in the refrigerator. Making the Chicken Stock and blending it with the vegetables (as in Step 1 below) requires very little tending, although it does require some time, so I often make the soup without the dumplings when I'm home doing other things, or at night. Then, I can whip up a quick batch of dumplings any time and cook them in the soup that's already been made. Just be sure to use a pot that is big enough for the dumplings to have room to swim around while they cook. They swell quite a bit.

1 recipe **Chicken Stock**, including chicken and vegetables (page 35)
1 cup all-purpose gluten-free flour
½ teaspoon xanthan gum
2 teaspoons baking powder
½ teaspoon kosher salt
1 cup milk (low-fat is fine, nonfat is not)

1. After making the Chicken Stock, remove the pot from the stove top. Remove and discard the bay leaf. Skim any impurities off the top of the pot and discard. Remove the chicken and set it aside. Using an immersion blender, blend the vegetables used to make the stock into the liquid. Blend until no large pieces remain. Return the pot to the stove top, and turn the heat to medium-high. Cover partially and allow the liquid to simmer.

2. In a separate medium-size bowl, blend the flour, xanthan gum, baking powder, and salt until well combined. Add the milk in a slow, steady stream, whisking as you go. Continue to whisk until the batter is smooth.

3. Remove the cover from the pot, and drop the dumpling batter by the heaping tablespoonful into the simmering soup, pausing in between tablespoonfuls to allow the dumplings to maintain space between one another. The dumplings swell as they cook. Cover the pot partially and allow the dumplings to simmer until they are cooked through, 7 to 10 minutes.

4. While the dumplings are cooking, remove the skin and bones from the cooked chicken and shred the meat.

5. Serve by ladling the soup into bowls, 2 dumplings per bowl, and topping with ½ cup shredded chicken. Serve immediately.

"Matzoh" Ball Soup

MAKES 4 TO 5 SERVINGS

The next time someone in your family is under the weather, try making him or her a fresh batch of this "matzoh" ball soup. Instead of matzoh meal (the finely ground matzoh that serves as the base of many Passover dishes), it's made with quinoa flakes (which you can find at most health food stores, and many supermarkets), which means that it is not only fortified with the usual loving kindness that comes in a warm, comforting bowl of matzoh ball soup, but it also has tons of protein. So rest up and take care. Eat, eat! You're skin and bones.

3 extra-large eggs

¼ cup vegetable oil

1 teaspoon kosher salt

Freshly ground black pepper, to taste

1 cup quinoa flakes (plus more, if necessary, by the tablespoon)

¼ cup all-purpose gluten-free flour

½ teaspoon xanthan gum

8 cups **Chicken Stock** (page 35)

1. In a large bowl, whisk the eggs, oil, salt, and pepper until well beaten. Add the quinoa flakes, flour, and xanthan gum and beat the mixture until it becomes thicker and a bit more elastic. If the mixture seems too squishy, add more quinoa flakes, by the tablespoon, until it becomes thick. Cover the bowl with plastic wrap and refrigerate for 30 minutes to an hour, until firm.

2. Once the mixture is firm, bring a large pot of salted water to a rolling boil. The "matzoh" balls are boiled in water, instead of in soup, because water allows them to move more freely when they cook, permitting them to cook fully, all the way through to the center of each one. Remove the batter from the refrigerator and, with wet hands, divide the mixture into 10 to 12 portions, and create round shapes of the portions by rolling them between wet palms. They will expand as they cook.

3. Carefully add the balls to the pot of boiling water, return to a rolling boil, cover the pot and boil the "matzoh" balls for 25 to 30 minutes, or until they are cooked through. The "matzoh" balls should allow a fork to pierce toward the center of each without too much resistance. Take care not to cook so long that they begin to fall apart in the pot.

4. In a separate large pot, heat the Chicken Stock until simmering. Serve the "matzoh" balls in steaming bowls of chicken soup.

Pot Roast

MAKES 5 TO 6 SERVINGS

Pot roast is a delightfully down-home dinner. Since it's cooked in such delicious-ness for such a long time, it is foolproof to make. It can be served up simply by slicing it against the grain and drizzling it with pan juices alongside some boiled potatoes and fresh asparagus, or you can shred it with your hands and use it to make beef tacos or fajitas. You can also save whatever liquid you don't use for serving the pot roast, with all its flavors and bits and pieces of beef, and use it in place of water to make delicious brown rice. Just cook the rice accord-ing to the package directions, substituting the reserved liquid for water, one-for-one.

2 tablespoons extra-virgin olive oil

4 shallots (or 1 large yellow onion), diced

4 cloves of garlic, crushed and peeled

1 tablespoon red chile powder

2 tablespoons ground cumin

2 pounds beef brisket, trimmed of excess fat

2 tablespoons kosher salt

1 tablespoon freshly ground black pepper

1 (28-ounce) can whole, peeled tomatoes, chopped

2 cups **Chicken Stock** (page 35)

1. In a large Dutch oven, drizzle the olive oil in the bottom of the pot and turn the heat to medium-high. Add the shallots and garlic and cook, stirring fre-quently, until the shallots are translucent and the garlic is fragrant (6 to 7 min-utes). Add the chile powder and cumin and stir to combine.

2. Place the brisket in the pot, and season it on all sides with the salt and pepper. Brown the brisket by rotating it in the hot pan, cooking it for about 3 to 5 minutes per side. Once the beef is browned, add the tomatoes and Chicken Stock, then enough water to cover the meat. Bring the liquid to a boil, then re-

duce it to a simmer, cover with the lid, and cook until the meat is very tender and begins to fall apart, about 3½ hours.

3. Once the meat is cool enough to handle, remove it from the pan and allow it to rest for 30 minutes before slicing with a knife (against the grain) or shredding with your hands.

Sweet and Sour Chicken

MAKES 6 TO 8 SERVINGS

When skinless, boneless chicken breast is on sale, I buy lots of it, clean it up, cut some into strips, some into chunks, divide the meat into groups of four to five portions, and freeze each portion in a separate, freezer-safe plastic storage bag. When I am ready to use a portion, I defrost it in the refrigerator overnight. I am always experimenting with different chicken dishes that are interesting and tasty without being fried. This sweet and sour chicken tastes remarkably like take-out, without the price tag and without the MSG.

2 pounds skinless, boneless chicken breast, cut into bite-size chunks (about 1½ inch square)

2 tablespoons gluten-free soy sauce (I like La Choy Lite)

2 tablespoons cornstarch

¼ teaspoon freshly ground black pepper

3 tablespoons sesame or canola oil

5 cloves garlic, crushed and peeled

2 carrots, peeled and cut into 1½-inch chunks

2 sweet bell peppers (any color), seeded and cut into 1½-inch chunks

4 scallions, trimmed and chopped (cross-sections)

1 recipe **Sweet and Sour Sauce**, at room temperature (page 53)

1. In a large bowl, toss the chicken, soy sauce, cornstarch, and pepper until all the pieces of chicken are coated. In a large, nonstick skillet over medium-high heat, heat the oil and simmer the crushed garlic for 2 to 3 minutes until it is fragrant and beginning to soften. Add the chicken to the pan and cook, in two batches if necessary, depending upon the size of the skillet, for 5 to 7 minutes, or until lightly browned and cooked through. Remove the chicken from the pan, draining and leaving behind in the pan as much liquid as possible, and set it aside in a separate medium-size bowl.

2. Add the carrots and peppers to the pan and cook over medium-high heat in the liquid until softened, 4 to 5 minutes. Lower the heat and return the chicken

mixture to the pan. Add the scallions and the Sweet and Sour Sauce to the pan and cook over low heat for 2 to 3 minutes, until the ingredients are well combined and the sauce is heated through. Serve immediately over cooked rice.

Shoestring Savings

Sweet and Sour Chicken

On a shoestring: $8.05 for about 7 servings

If you bought it: $36.33 for 7 servings (frozen)

Asian Pork Loin

MAKES 4 SERVINGS

This recipe makes enough marinade to cook a vegetable, like chopped carrots or shredded cabbage, in the roasting pan with the pork. The meat will be so soft and moist, you can even shred it if you like. I like to buy a large, 4-pound pork loin when it is on sale, slice it in half, and marinate each of the 2 pounds according to this recipe in separate plastic bags (doubling the marinade). Once the meat has finished marinating, freeze one of the 2-pound packages, marinade and all. When you are ready to use the frozen and prepared pork loin, allow it to defrost in the refrigerator overnight and then roast it according to the recipe directions. You'll be so glad you did.

½ cup gluten-free soy sauce (I like La-Choy Lite)

½ cup canola or sesame oil

3 tablespoons Worcestershire sauce

⅓ cup packed light brown sugar

2 tablespoons unsulphured molasses

1 teaspoon black peppercorns (or 1½ teaspoons freshly ground black pepper)

3 tablespoons fresh ginger, minced

4 tablespoons rice vinegar

4 tablespoons balsamic vinegar

2 leeks, trimmed and sliced thinly in cross-section

4 cloves of garlic, crushed and peeled

2 pounds pork loin, trimmed of the largest pieces of fat

1. In a large bowl, prepare the marinade by whisking the soy sauce, oil, Worcestershire sauce, sugar, molasses, pepper, ginger, vinegars, leeks, and garlic until well combined.

2. Place the trimmed pork loin into a large, resealable plastic bag, pour the marinade into the bag on top of the meat, and seal the bag securely. With the bag sealed, gently massage the contents until the marinade has covered the

meat completely. Place the bag, seam side up, in a large bowl and place the bowl in the refrigerator.

3. Allow the meat to marinate for at least 2 hours, and then turn the bag over so the other side of the meat is sitting in the marinade. Keep in the refrigerator for at least another 4 hours, or overnight.

4. Once the meat has finished marinating, preheat the oven to 325°F. Place the meat and the marinade in a roasting pan and place in the center of the pre-heated oven and cook for approximately 90 minutes, or until the center of the roast reaches 160°F. Remove from the oven and allow the meat to rest for at least 10 to 15 minutes before slicing against the grain.

Eight

Room for Dessert: Cakes, Cookies, and Pies

Perfect Yellow Cupcakes

MAKES 12 CUPCAKES

These really are the perfect little yellow cupcakes. They are moist and super flavorful, with toothsome cupcake texture. You can also make a cake with the same recipe. Just bake the batter in a 9-inch round pan at 350°F for 20 minutes, and then 40 minutes at 300°F, until a toothpick inserted in the center comes out clean. For the ideal cupcake experience, frost with **Sour Cream Chocolate Frosting** (page 240).

1 stick (8 tablespoons) unsalted butter, at room temperature

1 cup sugar

2 extra-large eggs, at room temperature

1½ teaspoons pure vanilla extract

1½ cups all-purpose gluten-free flour

¾ teaspoon xanthan gum

1½ teaspoons baking powder

½ teaspoon kosher salt

1 cup plus 2 tablespoons milk, at room temperature (low-fat is fine, nonfat is not)

1. Preheat your oven to 350°F. Grease or line a standard twelve-cup muffin pan with unsalted butter and set it aside.

2. In a large bowl, cream the butter and sugar until light and fluffy. Add the eggs one at a time, beating well after each addition until smooth. Add the vanilla and stir to combine. To the wet ingredients, add the flour, xanthan gum, baking powder, and salt, beating well after each addition. Add the milk and beat the mixture until it becomes thicker and a bit more elastic (which will mean that the xanthan gum has been activated).

3. Distribute the batter evenly among the twelve muffin cups. Place the muffin tin in the preheated oven and bake for 25 minutes, or until the cupcakes are pale golden and a toothpick inserted into the center of a middle muffin cup comes out clean.

Shoestring Savings

Perfect Yellow Cupcakes

On a shoestring: 25¢ per cupcake

If you bought it: $2.00 per cupcake (frozen)

Chocolate-Chip Blondie Cupcakes

MAKES 12 CUPCAKES

The brown sugar in these blonde-brownie cupcakes makes them a denser and more decadent alternative to traditional vanilla and chocolate cupcakes.

1 stick (8 tablespoons) unsalted butter, at room temperature

1½ cups packed brown sugar

2 extra-large eggs

2 teaspoons pure vanilla extract

2 cups all-purpose gluten-free flour

1 teaspoon xanthan gum

½ teaspoon baking soda

½ teaspoon kosher salt

12 ounces semi-sweet chocolate chips

1. Preheat your oven to 350°F. Grease a standard twelve-cup muffin pan with unsalted butter and set it aside.

2. In a large bowl, beat the butter and sugar together until light and fluffy. Add the eggs, one at a time, and the vanilla, blending well after each addition.

3. To the large bowl of wet ingredients, add the flour, xanthan gum, baking soda, and salt, reserving a few tablespoons of the dry ingredients in a small bowl, and blend the mixture well. Beat the batter well until it becomes thicker and a bit more elastic. Add the chocolate chips to the reserved dry ingredients and toss to coat them, then add them to the batter and stir to distribute the chips evenly throughout the batter.

4. Spoon the batter into the prepared muffin pan, dividing it evenly among the cups. The batter should be thick and stiff. If it doesn't seem thick enough, add an additional tablespoon or two of flour. If the batter is too moist, the cupcakes will puff, and then cave in on themselves. They'll still taste good, but you'll be sad. And so will your cupcakes.

5. Place the muffin pan in the preheated oven and bake for 20 to 25 minutes, until a toothpick inserted in the center of a cupcake comes out clean.

Lemon Cupcakes

MAKES 12 CUPCAKES

These cupcakes are a refreshing alternative to yellow cupcakes, with or without the **Citrus Glaze** (page 239). Since they are very moist, they freeze quite nicely, so there are always a few of these in our deep freezer. When I get last-minute notice of an upcoming birthday party in my son's school, I just grab one of these out of the freezer, stick it in a container, and stash it in his backpack without even defrosting it. It's ready to go when the party gets started.

1 stick (8 tablespoons) unsalted butter, at room temperature

1 cup sugar

2 extra-large eggs

1½ teaspoons pure vanilla extract

Zest and juice of 1 lemon (reserve 1–2 tablespoons for glaze)

1½ cups all-purpose gluten-free flour

¾ teaspoon xanthan gum

2 teaspoons baking powder

½ teaspoon kosher salt

½ cup sour cream (low-fat is fine, nonfat is not)

Shoestring Savings

Lemon Cupcakes

On a shoestring: $0.33 per cupcake

If you bought it: $2.00 per cupcake (frozen)

1. Preheat your oven to 350°F. Grease a standard twelve-cup muffin tin with unsalted butter and set it aside.

2. In a large bowl, combine butter and sugar until light and fluffy. Add the eggs, one at a time, then the vanilla, and the lemon zest and juice (reserving the final 1 to 2 tablespoons of juice for the glaze), blending well after each addition. Add the flour, xanthan gum, baking powder, and salt, and beat to combine. Once the final ingredients have been added, beat the mixture until it becomes thicker and a bit more elastic (which means that the xanthan gum has been activated). Add the sour cream to the batter and mix until well combined.

3. Divide the batter evenly among the muffin cups and bake in the center of the preheated oven for about 25 minutes, until a toothpick inserted into the center of a cupcake comes out clean. Cool for 5 minutes in the tin and then transfer to a wire rack to cool completely.

4. Serve glazed cupcakes chilled. Serve plain cupcakes at room temperature.

Pound Cake

MAKES 1 LOAF OF POUND CAKE

This pound cake may remind you of a certain brand-name pound cake that can be found in the freezer aisle. Packaged in a foil pan with a cardboard cover, it was always in my sweet-toothed grandmother's freezer (I realize that the part about my grandmother is not a helpful part of the hint for most of you). But this one's gluten-free, and you can make it at home for a fraction of the cost. It can be made up to 3 days ahead of time, wrapped tightly, and stored at room temperature until ready to serve. It also freezes quite well and can even be drizzled with **Citrus Glaze** (page 239).

This cake does take some patience when it comes to baking it in the oven, so just plan to make this when you're already doing other things puttering around the kitchen. (Better yet, double the recipe to make two, and stick one in the freezer.) The precise oven temperatures are all in the name of coaxing the batter into a smooth loaf that is not cracked. So put on your kid gloves and get ready for a nice, satisfying slice of my grandmother's pound cake.

1½ sticks (12 tablespoons) unsalted butter, at room temperature

4 ounces cream cheese, at room temperature

1½ cups sugar

3 extra-large eggs, at room temperature

1 tablespoon pure vanilla extract

1½ cups all-purpose gluten-free flour

¾ teaspoon xanthan gum

1 teaspoon kosher salt

1. Grease well with unsalted butter a loaf pan that is no larger than 9 x 5 inches. We begin this recipe with a cold oven, so no preheating this time.

2. In a large bowl, cream together the butter, cream cheese, and sugar until light and fluffy. Add the eggs one at a time, beating well after each addition. Add the vanilla and blend.

3. Add the flour, xanthan gum, and salt to the wet ingredients and blend well until the batter becomes thicker and a bit more elastic. Pour the batter into the prepared loaf pan, smooth the top, and tap the pan flat on the counter to break any air bubbles that may have formed beneath the surface.

4. Place the pan in the center of a cold oven. Set the temperature of the oven to 200°F and bake for 20 minutes. Next, increase the temperature to 250°F and bake for 20 minutes more. Then increase the temperature to 275°F and bake for 10 minutes. Finally, raise the temperature to 300°F and bake for 1 hour longer, or until a tester inserted into the center comes out clean.

Devil's Food Cake (or Snack Cakes)

MAKES 6 SERVINGS

If a devil's food snack cake is what you crave, a snack cake you should have. Simply bake this cake in a square pan. While the cake is cooling, whip up a batch of the filling from our **Chocolate Sandwich Cookies** (page 205). Once the cake has cooled, turn it over and slice it carefully in the middle with a large serrated knife, creating two equal rectangles. Spread the sandwich cookie filling evenly over the bottom of one of the rectangles, top with the other rectangle, and slice into individual snack cakes. If you get caught in the act, just say, "the Devil made me do it."

1 stick (8 tablespoons) unsalted butter, at room temperature

1½ cups packed brown sugar

2 extra-large eggs

1 teaspoon pure vanilla extract

½ cup sour cream

2 cups all-purpose gluten-free flour

1 teaspoon xanthan gum

¾ cup unsweetened Dutch-processed cocoa powder

1¼ teaspoons baking soda

¾ teaspoon kosher salt

1⅓ cups water

1. Preheat oven to 350°F. Grease an 8- or 9-inch square or round pan with unsalted butter and set it aside. Using a springform pan will ensure easy removal of the cake from the pan, but it's really not necessary.

2. In a large bowl, cream the butter and sugar together until light and fluffy. Add the eggs, one at a time, then the vanilla and sour cream, blending well after each addition.

3. To the large bowl of wet ingredients, add the flour, xanthan gum, cocoa powder, baking soda, and salt and blend well. Add the water and beat the batter well until it becomes thicker and a bit more elastic. Pour batter into the prepared pan.

4. Place the cake pan in the center of the preheated oven and bake for 45 to 55 minutes, until a toothpick inserted in the center comes out clean, maybe with a few moist crumbs attached. The cake should be a little spongy, not dense. Do not overbake.

Shoestring Savings

Devil's Food Cake

On a shoestring: $4.32 for 6 servings

If you bought a mix (and still made it yourself):
$11.00 for 6 servings

Perfect Chocolate Birthday Cake

MAKES 1 ROUND CAKE

This cake is a real crowd-pleaser. Everyone seems to be able to agree upon it. Although it seems a bit like a flourless chocolate cake, it's not quite as rich as that, and not quite as dense. It's ready for anything, including a birthday message. Just cool completely, glaze with warm **Chocolate Ganache** (page 236), place it in the refrigerator for an hour so the glaze will harden, write your message, and serve chilled.

1½ sticks (12 tablespoons) unsalted butter, at room temperature

1 cup sugar

3 extra-large eggs

1 teaspoon pure vanilla extract

¾ cup all-purpose gluten-free flour

½ teaspoon xanthan gum

¾ cup unsweetened Dutch-processed cocoa powder

½ teaspoon baking powder

¼ teaspoon kosher salt

½ cup sour cream (low-fat is fine, nonfat is not)

1. Preheat oven to 350°F. Grease an 8-inch round cake pan with unsalted butter, line it with parchment paper, and grease the parchment paper. I like to use a springform pan because I can release the sides right as it comes out of the oven, and it cools faster, but you can do without it, for sure. Set aside the prepared pan.

2. In a large bowl, beat the butter and sugar together until light and fluffy. Add the eggs, one at a time, and the vanilla, blending well after each addition.

3. To the large bowl of wet ingredients, add the flour, xanthan gum, cocoa powder, baking powder, and salt and blend the mixture well. Add the sour cream and beat the batter well until it becomes thicker and a bit more elastic. Pour the batter into the prepared pan, smooth the top, and tap the pan on the countertop to break up any air bubbles that may have formed.

4. Place the pan in the preheated oven and bake for 30 to 35 minutes, until a toothpick inserted in the center comes out clean. Remove the pan from the oven. If you used a springform pan, pop open the sides a few minutes after you take it out of the oven. If not, leave it be. Either way, allow the cake to cool for at least 15 minutes before inverting it onto a wire rack to cool completely.

Apple Cake

MAKES 12 TO 15 SQUARES OF APPLE CAKE

A nice warm, buttery apple cake like this one is an essential part of your reper-toire. It's less iconic than an apple pie and not quite as effortless to throw to-gether as apple crisp. However, you'll find that people tend to fall naturally into three separate and distinct categories: you have your crisp people, your pie peo-ple, and your cake people. I want to make sure that like a Boy (or Girl) Scout, you're prepared for any eventuality.

CAKE

1½ sticks (12 tablespoons) unsalted butter, at room temperature

1½ cups granulated sugar

2 extra-large eggs

1 tablespoon pure vanilla extract

2 cups all-purpose gluten-free flour

1 teaspoon xanthan gum

1 teaspoon baking soda

¼ teaspoon kosher salt

2 teaspoons ground cinnamon

⅓ cup sour cream (low-fat is fine, nonfat is not)

FILLING

3–4 McIntosh apples, peeled, cored, and sliced thin (about 2 cups)

5 tablespoons granulated sugar

5 tablespoons brown sugar

2 teaspoons ground cinnamon

¼ teaspoon kosher salt

1 teaspoon cornstarch

1. Preheat your oven to 325°F. Line a 9 x 13-inch baking dish with parchment paper and set it aside.

2. **To make the cake:** In a large bowl, cream the butter and sugar until light and fluffy. Add the eggs and vanilla and beat to combine. Add the flour, xanthan gum, baking soda, salt, and cinnamon, beating well after each addition. Add the sour cream and blend. Beat the batter well until it becomes thicker and a bit more elastic. Set aside the cake batter to prepare the filling.

3. **To make the filling:** In a separate, medium-size bowl, place the apples, sugars, cinnamon, salt, and cornstarch, and stir to combine well.

4. Layer one half the cake batter evenly in the prepared baking dish, then layer in the filling mixture and top evenly with the remaining cake batter, smoothing the top with wet hands.

5. Place the baking dish in the center of the preheated oven and bake for 45 minutes to 1 hour, or until a toothpick inserted in the center comes out clean.

6. Cool completely in the dish. Remove the cake from the pan and slice it into squares with a serrated knife.

Pumpkin Chocolate Chip Squares

MAKES ABOUT 18 SQUARES

I came close to setting this recipe aside, thinking that we had enough pumpkin-laden, Thanksgiving-themed recipes for one cookbook. And then one day my son asked my husband what his favorite dessert was. Imagine my surprise when he answered, "Pumpkin Chocolate Chip Squares." So that settled it. These squares are worth squirreling away a few cans of packed pumpkin in the fall for other times of year. Pumpkin pairs remarkably well with chocolate. Try to resist the (understandable) temptation, though, to add more pumpkin than the recipe calls for. It really throws off the moisture balance in the squares and makes them gooey, but in a bad way.

2 sticks (16 tablespoons) unsalted butter, at room temperature

1¼ cups sugar

1 extra-large egg, beaten

2 teaspoons pure vanilla extract

1 cup canned solid pumpkin

2 cups all-purpose gluten-free flour

1 teaspoon xanthan gum

1 tablespoon pumpkin pie spice

1 teaspoon baking soda

¾ teaspoon kosher salt

1 (12-ounce) package semi-sweet chocolate chips

1. Preheat the oven to 350°F. Line a 9 x 13-inch baking pan with parchment paper, allowing the lining to overhang the edges.

2. In a large bowl, cream the butter and sugar until light and fluffy. Add the egg, then the vanilla and pumpkin, and beat to combine. Add the flour, xanthan gum, pumpkin pie spice, baking soda, and salt, beating after each addition and reserving a couple tablespoons of the flour in a small bowl. Beat the batter well until it becomes thicker and a bit more elastic. Add the chocolate chips to the

small bowl of reserved flour, and toss to coat. Then add the flour-coated chips to the batter and stir until the chips are evenly distributed throughout.

3. Pour the batter into the prepared baking pan, smoothing the top. Place the pan in the preheated oven and bake for 35 to 40 minutes, or until a toothpick inserted into the center of the pan comes out clean.

4. After cooling completely in the pan, lift out the squares by the overhung parchment paper. Peel back the parchment paper, and slice into squares with a serrated knife.

Pumpkin Bread

MAKES 1 LOAF

This is a very moist and flavorful quick bread that is great for Thanksgiving but works all year round. All you have to do is stock up on packed pumpkin in November, and you'll be ready at a moment's notice, any time of year.

Scant 2 cups all-purpose gluten-free flour

1 teaspoon xanthan gum

¾ cup sugar

¾ cup gluten-free oats

1½ teaspoons baking soda

1 teaspoon ground cinnamon

1½ cups canned packed pumpkin

¾ cup pure maple syrup

⅛ cup canola oil (plus more for greasing the pan)

2 extra-large egg whites, beaten

7 prunes (dried plums), pureed in 2 to 3 tablespoons water

½ cup raisins (soaked in warm water for 15 minutes, then drained)

1. Preheat oven to 350°F. Grease well with canola oil a 9 x 5-inch loaf pan and set it aside.

2. In a large bowl, place the flour, xanthan gum, sugar, oats, baking soda, and cinnamon. Whisk to combine. Add the pumpkin, maple syrup, oil, egg whites, and pureed prunes to the dry ingredients one at a time, blending well after each addition. After the last addition, blend well until the batter becomes thicker and a bit more elastic. Add the raisins and mix to combine.

3. Pour the batter into the greased loaf pan and smooth the top. Place in the preheated oven and bake for about 1 hour, until a toothpick inserted into the center of the loaf pan comes out clean.

Lady Fingers

MAKES ABOUT 12 LADY FINGERS

Lady fingers are not just for ladies. And they're not actual fingers. They're just vaguely reminiscent of fingers in their shape. They are delicate and lightly sweet, with a thin crispy outside and a light and cakey inside, like angel food cake. These elegant little cookies are easy on the wallet, too, because they don't use much flour.

4 extra-large eggs, separated carefully into yolks and whites

Dash (⅛ teaspoon) cream of tartar

½ cup confectioner's sugar

¾ cup all-purpose gluten-free flour

Scant ½ teaspoon xanthan gum

Pinch (½ dash) kosher salt

1½ teaspoons pure vanilla extract

1. Preheat the oven to 325°F. Line two baking sheets with parchment paper and set them aside.

2. In the bowl of your stand mixer fitted with the whisk attachment, beat the egg whites and the cream of tartar until they form stiff peaks. If they don't become stiff, there is almost certainly some yolk in the whites. Once the whites have become stiff, gently scrape them out of the bowl of the mixer into another medium bowl and set them aside.

3. In your stand mixer once again, with the same whisk attachment (the danger is yolk in the whites, not vice versa), mix the egg yolks and the sugar for 8 to 10 minutes on at least medium speed, until pale yellow, thick, and nearly tripled in volume.

4. Into the yolk mixture, gently fold the flour, xanthan gum, salt, and vanilla and then the egg white mixture, until smooth.

5. Fill a pastry bag fitted with a ¾ inch plain tip (in a pinch, you could use a zipper-style plastic sandwich bag and cut a hole in the corner) with the dough. Pipe fingers about 4 inches long, 2 inches apart, on the prepared baking sheets. Place the baking sheets in the preheated oven and bake for about 12 to 15 minutes, until pale golden on the outside, rotating the sheets halfway through baking.

Black & White Cookies

MAKES ABOUT 16 COOKIES

These cookies are a New York favorite, and whenever I see anyone try to pass off a cookie as a Black & White when it is frosted, rather than iced, I take personal offense. The icing should be thick enough that it dries opaque, but thin enough that it dribbles slowly off a spoon. You'll need to make the cookies well in advance of icing them, because they must be completely cool or the icing will stay wet and weepy, and you won't get a smooth finish because the cookies will crumble when you try to ice them. The cookies themselves are worth eating on their own, but nothing compares to a beautiful, iced Black & White.

COOKIE

5 tablespoons unsalted butter, at room temperature

½ cup sugar

1 extra-large egg

½ teaspoon pure vanilla extract

⅓ cup sour cream (low-fat is fine, nonfat is not)

1¼ cups all-purpose gluten-free flour

Heaping ½ teaspoon xanthan gum

½ teaspoon baking soda

½ teaspoon kosher salt

ICING

1½ cups confectioner's sugar (plus more by the tablespoon)

1 tablespoon light corn syrup

1 teaspoon freshly squeezed lemon juice

¼ teaspoon vanilla extract

1–2 tablespoons water

¼ cup unsweetened Dutch-processed cocoa powder

1. Preheat your oven to 350°F. Line rimmed baking sheets with parchment paper and set them aside.

2. Beat the butter and sugar in a large bowl until light and fluffy. Add the egg, then the sour cream and vanilla, beating well in between each addition. Add the flour, xanthan gum, baking soda, and salt and mix to combine. Beat the batter well until it becomes thicker and a bit more elastic. Chill the batter before baking it to keep the cookies from spreading too much. Spoon the chilled batter onto the lined baking sheets by the heaping tablespoonful, about 2 inches apart. Bake until the cookie tops are puffed and pale golden, about 15 minutes. Cool completely.

3. To make the icing, stir together the confectioner's sugar, corn syrup, lemon juice, vanilla, and about 1 tablespoon of water in a small bowl until completely smooth (this makes the white icing). Transfer half the icing into another bowl, add the cocoa, and stir very well (this makes the black icing). Add water by the tablespoonful to thin (and more confectioner's sugar to thicken, also by the tablespoonful) both the black and the white icing separately, stirring very well after each addition. The consistency should be such that it dribbles from a spoon gracefully, like molasses.

4. To ice the cookies, turn them flat side up, and spread the white icing over half and the black over the other half. The icing should be thick enough that it doesn't melt into the cookie when you spread it. If it disappears, add some more confectioner's sugar and stir to thicken. Serve chilled, so the icing is set just right.

Shoestring Savings

Black & White Cookies

On a shoestring: $3.00 for 16 cookies

If you bought it: $16.00 for 16 cookies

Chocolate Chip Cookies

MAKES 2 DOZEN COOKIES

It's really important to keep this batter cold before you bake these cookies. That will keep them from spreading too much. You can either refrigerate the dough for an hour or so before baking or just stick the cookie sheets with the dough on them in the freezer for about 15 minutes before baking. The warmer the climate where you're baking, the longer you should refrigerate or freeze the dough before baking.

1 stick unsalted butter (8 tablespoons), at room temperature

¾ cup granulated sugar

¾ cup packed brown sugar

2 extra-large eggs

1 tablespoon pure vanilla extract

2¼ cups all-purpose gluten-free flour

1¼ teaspoons xanthan gum

½ teaspoon kosher salt

1 teaspoon baking soda

12 ounces semi-sweet chocolate chips

1. Preheat the oven to 350°F. Line rimmed baking sheets with parchment paper and set them aside.

2. In a large bowl, beat the butter and sugars until light and fluffy. Beat in the eggs, one at a time, and the vanilla until well blended. Add the flour, xanthan gum, salt, and baking soda to the wet ingredients, reserving a few tablespoons of dry ingredients. Beat the batter well until it becomes thicker and a bit more elastic.

3. In a small bowl, mix those few reserved tablespoons of dry ingredients with the chocolate chips and toss to coat. Stir the chocolate chips and the remaining dry ingredients into the cookie dough until they are evenly distributed. The dough should be very stiff and thick.

4. Drop balls of dough about 1¼ inches in diameter about 2 inches apart on lined baking sheets. Place the baking sheets with the cookie dough on them into the refrigerator to chill for about 15 minutes. Once the dough has chilled, place the rimmed baking sheets in the preheated oven and bake for 7 to 10 minutes. The cookies may seem undercooked. As long as the edges are beginning to brown and the cookies are lightly browned, they're done. They will firm up. Cool on the sheets for 10 minutes or until firm, then transfer to a wire rack to cool completely.

Shoestring Savings

Chocolate Chip Cookies

On a shoestring: $2.89 per dozen cookies

If you bought it: $7.00 per dozen cookies

Butter Cookies

MAKES ABOUT 4 DOZEN COOKIES, DEPENDING UPON SIZE

Butter cookies are lovely, delicate little creations, perfect for high tea and stuff (and an amazing **Cheesecake** crust, page 226). Years ago, I thought it would be brilliant to cut this dough with cookie cutters in the shape of letters in order to spell out a congratulatory message to one of my children. It wasn't. So if you ever find yourself in need of cookies as a means of communication, use **Sugar Cookies** (page 208) instead. They're much more robust. You could probably even write a short story out of sugar cookies. Butter cookies are more refined, so be kind to them.

2 sticks unsalted butter (16 tablespoons), at room temperature

⅔ cup superfine sugar (or grind 1 cup granulated sugar in a food processor for 15 seconds, and then measure out ⅔ cup, as ground)

2 teaspoons pure vanilla extract

2 cups all-purpose gluten-free flour

1 teaspoon xanthan gum

¼ teaspoon kosher salt

1. In a large bowl, blend the butter, sugar, and vanilla until just combined. This time, you don't want it to be light and fluffy. You want it flat. Add the flour, xanthan gum, and salt and beat until well blended. Wrap the dough in plastic wrap and place it in the refrigerator to cool for at least 1 hour until firm.

2. When you're ready to make the cookies, preheat the oven to 325°F. Line baking sheets with parchment paper and set them aside.

3. Let the dough sit out on the counter, still covered, for about 10 minutes until it softens slightly. Once it has begun to soften, cut the dough into four parts. Place one-quarter of the dough in between two sheets of plastic wrap and roll out until it's about ¼ inch thick. Release the dough from both sides of the plastic wrap by pulling off the top layer of plastic first, then replacing it. Now flip the dough over and remove the other layer of plastic wrap. Use cookie cutters in whatever shape you like, cutting as close together as possible. If the dough is

really soft, without pulling off the scraps in between the shapes, cover with the top plastic wrap again and place the dough gently in the freezer for a few minutes to firm it back up.

4. Remove dough from the freezer, pull off the scraps, gently remove the shapes, and place on prepared baking sheets about 1 inch apart. If necessary, place cookie sheets with dough on them in the freezer for a few minutes before baking. Next, place in the preheated oven for about 20 minutes, until the edges are golden.

5. Allow the cookies to rest on the cookie sheets for 5 to 10 minutes before transferring them to wire racks to cool completely.

Shoestring Savings

Butter Cookies

On a shoestring: 7¢ per cookie

If you bought it: 42¢ per cookie ($3.79 for a
   box of 9 cookies)

Chocolate Chip Butter Cookies

MAKES 2 DOZEN "COOKIES," MORE OR LESS

These cookies taste even better frozen. Eaten right from the bag. Before the freezer door closes. (Hypothetically.) And they can be made super quick, so they're a great thing to throw together if you are looking for a last-minute host(ess) gift to bring to someone's house. Just don't forget to suggest to your host(ess) that he or she siphon off a few and stick 'em in the freezer for late-night hankerings.

1½ sticks (12 tablespoons) unsalted butter, at room temperature

1 cup sugar

½ teaspoon kosher salt

1 teaspoon pure vanilla extract

2 cups all-purpose gluten-free flour

1 teaspoon xanthan gum

8 ounces semi-sweet chocolate chips

1. Preheat the oven to 350°F. Line a 9 x 13-inch rimmed baking sheet with parchment paper and set it aside.

2. In a large bowl, beat the butter and sugar until light and fluffy. Add the salt and vanilla and beat to combine. Add the flour and xanthan gum to the batter, reserving a few tablespoons of the flour. Toss the chocolate chips in the reserved flour until the chips are coated. The dough should stick together well when pressed in your palm. Add the chocolate chips and reserved flour to the batter and stir until the chips are evenly distributed throughout the dough.

3. Press the dough into the prepared baking sheet, ensuring it all sticks together, and then place it in the center of the preheated oven. Bake for 12 to 15 minutes, or until just beginning to brown around the edges. Allow the panel of cookies to cool completely on the sheet before breaking it into irregular shapes.

Chocolate Sandwich Cookies

MAKES ABOUT 30 COOKIES

These otherwise simple cookies have a big "wow" factor. They're addictive, but not in the same way as a certain famous chocolate sandwich cookie. Eating an entire sleeve of those cookies makes me feel vaguely ashamed. But baking and then eating a bunch of these, the homemade gluten-free version, makes me feel clever, ingenious even.

½ stick (4 tablespoons) unsalted butter, at room temperature

4 tablespoons vegetable shortening

1¼ teaspoons pure vanilla extract

1–1½ cups confectioner's sugar

1 recipe **Chocolate Wafer Cookies** (page 212)

1. In a large bowl, mix the butter, shortening, and vanilla until well blended. Add the first 1 cup of confectioner's sugar and stir until the sugar is incorporated completely into the butter mixture. The filling should be thick and stiff. Add more confectioner's sugar, one tablespoon at a time, to reach the desired consistency.

2. Place one-half of the chocolate wafer cookies upside down on a level surface. Divide the filling among the cookies and flatten with wet hands or a spoon. Place the other half of the cookies right side up on top of the filling and press down gently to create sandwich cookies.

Shoestring Savings

Chocolate Sandwich Cookies

On a shoestring: $5.28 for 30 cookies

If you bought it: $7.50 for 30 cookies

Ginger Cookies

MAKES ABOUT 4 DOZEN COOKIES, DEPENDING UPON SIZE

The smell of these ginger cookies baking in the oven is epicurean and unmistakable. Whatever you do, though, don't try baking them at night when anyone in your house is meant to be sleeping. It will wake them up and make them demand cookies. And, really, who wants that? On the plus side, you can make these two ways: a bit thicker and they'll be chewy, thin and they'll turn out crispy. They work best for **Pumpkin Pie** crust (page 216) when they're crispy, but they may still be used even if they're on the chewier side. You're the boss.

1 stick plus 2 tablespoons unsalted butter (10 tablespoons), at room temperature

⅔ cup sugar

4 tablespoons molasses

1 extra-large egg

1 teaspoon pure vanilla extract

2 cups all-purpose gluten-free flour

1 teaspoon xanthan gum

1½ teaspoons baking soda

½ teaspoon kosher salt

2½ teaspoons ground cinnamon

1½ teaspoons ground ginger

1. In a large bowl, beat the butter and sugar until light and fluffy. Add the molasses, egg, and vanilla, one ingredient at a time, beating well after each addition. Add the flour, xanthan gum, baking soda, salt, cinnamon, and ginger to the wet ingredients, mixing to combine. Beat the batter well until it becomes thicker and a bit more elastic. The dough will be sticky.

2. Wrap the dough in plastic wrap and place it in the refrigerator until it is firm (a few hours or overnight).

3. When the dough is ready, preheat the oven to 350°F. Line rimmed baking sheets with parchment paper and set them aside. Slice off small pieces of dough,

moisten the palms of your hands, and roll the dough between your palms to form small balls that are about ½ inch in diameter.

4. Place the balls of dough on baking sheets 2 inches apart, and press them down with a spoon to flatten.

5. Bake for about 12 minutes, give or take, until browned. If you like them snappy, bake them 2 to 3 minutes more. If you prefer them chewy, bake them 2 to 3 minutes less, and allow them to cool completely before attempting to remove them from the baking sheet. Then peel away the parchment paper, rather than trying to pull the cookie off of it directly.

Shoestring Savings

Ginger Cookies

On a shoestring: 9¢ per cookie

If you bought it: $1.00 per cookie

Sugar Cookies

MAKES 2 TO 3 DOZEN COOKIES, DEPENDING UPON SIZE

My favorite sugar cookies are cut with a round 1½-inch cutter and treated to a light sprinkling of sugar right before they go into the oven. But this sturdy dough can keep pace with you, whatever size and shape you would like to make it. When my son wanted a cake shaped like a penguin for his sixth birthday, small rounds of sugar cookie dough baked and then covered with black **Royal Icing** (page 241) were the perfect eyes.

1 stick (8 tablespoons) unsalted butter, at room temperature

1 cup sugar

1 extra-large egg plus 1 extra-large egg white, at room temperature

1 teaspoon pure vanilla extract

2 cups all-purpose gluten-free flour

1 teaspoon xanthan gum

½ teaspoon baking powder

¼ teaspoon kosher salt

1. In a large bowl, blend the butter, sugar, egg and egg white, and vanilla until well combined. Add the flour, xanthan gum, baking powder, and salt, beating well after each addition. After adding the final ingredient, beat the mixture until it becomes thicker and a bit more elastic. Divide the dough into two equal parts, wrap each part in plastic wrap, and place the dough in the refrigerator to cool for at least 1 hour until firm.

2. Once the dough is properly chilled, preheat the oven to 350°F. Line baking sheets with parchment paper and set them aside.

3. For each portion of dough, wrap between two sheets of plastic wrap and roll out until it's about ¼ inch thick. Release the dough from both sides of the plastic wrap by pulling off the top layer of plastic first, then replacing it. Now flip the dough over and remove the other layer of plastic wrap. Use cookie cutters in whatever shape you like, cutting as close together as possible. If the dough is really soft, without pulling off the scraps in between the shapes, cover the top

with plastic wrap again and place the dough gently in the freezer for a few minutes to firm it up.

4. Once the dough has chilled, remove it from the freezer, pull off the scraps, gently remove the shapes, and place on prepared baking sheets about 1 inch apart. If necessary, place cookie sheets with dough on them in the freezer for a few minutes before baking. Next, place in the preheated oven for 7 to 12 minutes (shorter for chewier cookies, longer for crispier ones).

5. Allow to cool on the sheets for 5 minutes, then place on a wire rack to cool completely.

Shoestring Savings

Sugar Cookies

On a shoestring: $3.00 for about 30 cookies

If you bought it: $10.38 for 30 cookies

Butter-Pecan Cookies

MAKES 10 TO 12 COOKIES

Butter-pecan cookies are such a delightful buttery treat to serve with a warm cup of tea. I use pecan pieces, since they're much less expensive than whole pecans. I tend to make these in rounds, but they are also nice and fancy if you press the dough into a half-moon shape. Crumble them over vanilla ice cream for makeshift butter-pecan ice cream. The dough must be chilled before you put them in the oven to prevent spreading during baking.

½ cup pecan pieces
1 stick (8 tablespoons) unsalted butter, at room temperature
⅓ cup confectioner's sugar
1 teaspoon pure vanilla extract
⅛ teaspoon kosher salt
1 cup all-purpose gluten-free flour
½ teaspoon xanthan gum

1. In a small, dry, nonstick skillet, toast the pecan pieces over low heat for 3 to 5 minutes, or until lightly toasted and fragrant. Set them aside to cool.

2. In a large bowl, beat the butter, sugar, and vanilla until well combined. Add the salt, flour, and xanthan gum, reserving a tablespoon of the flour in a small bowl, beating well after each addition. Add the toasted, cooled pecans to the small bowl of reserved flour and toss them to coat. Add the pecans and re-served flour to the large bowl of cookie dough, and mix the dough until the pecans are evenly distributed throughout. Wrap the dough in plastic wrap, and place it in the refrigerator to cool for at least 1 hour until firm.

3. Once the dough is properly chilled, preheat your oven to 350°F. Line baking sheets with parchment paper and set them aside.

4. Divide the dough into ten to twelve pieces, rolling each piece between wet hands to create a ball, then flatten into disks. Place the flattened disks about 1 inch apart on prepared baking sheets and refrigerate again for 15 to 20 minutes.

5. Once the dough is chilled, place the baking sheets in the center of your preheated oven and bake for 12 to 15 minutes, or until golden brown around the edges. Remove the baking sheets from the oven and allow to cool on the sheets for 5 minutes before transferring to a wire rack to cool completely.

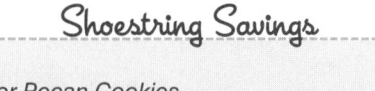

Butter-Pecan Cookies

On a shoestring: $2.42 for 10 cookies

If you bought it: $4.40 for 10 cookies

Chocolate Wafer Cookies

MAKES ABOUT 60 COOKIES, DEPENDING UPON SIZE

These chocolate wafer cookies are like the kind that tends to be sold in a sleeve, since they're delicate and can't be manhandled. They're fabulous alone, but are show-stoppers when they're used to make **Chocolate Sandwich Cookies** (page 205). I bet you could get your kids to eat all manner of vegetables just by dangling the promise of these babies at the end of a meal. Not that I've ever done that.

1 stick plus 6 tablespoons (14 tablespoons) unsalted butter, melted and cooled

1 cup sugar

1 extra-large egg

½ teaspoon pure vanilla extract

1¼ cups all-purpose gluten-free flour

1 teaspoon xanthan gum

½ cup unsweetened Dutch-processed cocoa powder

1 teaspoon baking soda

¼ teaspoon baking powder

¼ teaspoon kosher salt

1. In a large bowl, beat the butter and sugar until light and fluffy. Add the egg and vanilla, blending well after each addition. Add the flour, xanthan gum, cocoa powder, baking soda, baking powder, and salt, blending well after each addition. After adding the final ingredient, beat until the mixture becomes thicker and a bit more elastic.

2. Divide the dough into two equal portions, wrap each in plastic wrap, and refrigerate for at least 1 hour, or until firm. Line baking sheets with parchment paper and set them aside.

3. Once the dough has chilled, remove one of the dough portions from the refrigerator, place it between two sheets of plastic wrap, and roll into a round shape about ⅛ inch thick. Repeat with the other portion of the dough. Place all

of the dough back in the refrigerator, still wrapped in plastic wrap, and chill for another 15 to 20 minutes or until firm again.

4. Once the rolled-out dough is chilled, working with one portion at a time, remove and replace one piece of plastic wrap, and remove the plastic wrap from the other side. Using a 2-inch round cookie cutter, cut the dough into circles as close together as possible. Repeat the process with the other half of the dough. Gather the scraps of dough that remain, roll them flat again, chill, and cut more rounds.

5. Place the rounds about 1 inch apart on prepared baking sheets. Place the baking sheets in the refrigerator to chill while you preheat your oven to 325°F. Once the oven is ready, remove the baking sheets from the refrigerator, set them in the center of the preheated oven, and bake at 325°F for 5 minutes. Rotate the baking sheets 180 degrees and bake 4 to 6 minutes more, until the cookies are firm but not burned.

6. Cool the cookies for 5 to 10 minutes on the baking sheets. If they are too soft once they have cooled for 10 minutes, return them to the oven and bake for another couple minutes for that "snap." Once the cookies are baked and cooled enough to be firm, transfer them to a wire rack to cool completely.

Graham Crackers

MAKES ABOUT 16 GRAHAM CRACKERS, DEPENDING UPON SIZE AND SHAPE.
IT CAN BE DOUBLED EASILY.

Without graham crackers, there are no s'mores, and there is no graham cracker crust. Without graham cracker crust, you can't make a proper **Banana Cream Pie** (page 218). These crackers are lightly sweet, keep beautifully in the refrigerator, and can be made into any shape you like, although I keep it old school: perforated rectangles.

¼ cup (4 tablespoons) unsalted butter, at room temperature

4 tablespoons dark brown sugar

2 tablespoons granulated sugar

3 tablespoons honey

½ teaspoon pure vanilla extract

⅓ cup milk (low-fat is fine, nonfat is not)

1½ cups all-purpose gluten-free flour

¾ teaspoon xanthan gum

⅛ teaspoon kosher salt

¼ teaspoon baking soda

½ teaspoon baking powder

1. In a large bowl, or the bowl of your stand mixer fitted with the paddle attachment, cream the butter and both sugars until light and fluffy. Add the honey and the vanilla and then the milk, beating after each addition, until everything is well incorporated. Add the flour, xanthan gum, salt, baking soda, and baking powder and mix until well combined. Continue to beat the batter vigorously for another 3 to 4 minutes to activate the xanthan gum.

2. Divide the cracker dough into two parts, wrap each separately in plastic wrap, and chill in the refrigerator for at least 4 hours or overnight.

3. Once the dough has chilled, place one part of it between two pieces of plastic wrap and roll into a rectangle that is approximately 5 x 15 inches and about ⅛ inch thick. The thickness matters more than the size of the rectangle.

Place the rolled out dough back in the refrigerator on a flat surface and chill again for another 15 to 30 minutes until firm again. This little exercise will make the dough considerably easier to handle. Repeat with the other half of the dough.

4. While the dough is chilling for the second time, line rimmed baking sheets with parchment paper and preheat the oven to 350°F.

5. Once the dough has chilled again, score each rectangle with a sharp knife, separating the dough into whatever size rectangles you would like for the crackers. Separate the rectangles of dough from one another and place an inch or less apart on the prepared baking sheets (they won't spread much, if at all, during baking). If you like, mark a line down the center of each cookie and prick with a fork in a regular pattern.

6. Place the baking sheets in the preheated oven and bake at 350°F for about 10 minutes, until the crackers are crisp.

7. Remove the crackers from the oven and allow them to cool completely before handling them. They cool quickly right there on the baking sheets.

Pumpkin Pie with Ginger Cookie Crust

MAKES 8 SERVINGS

Say farewell to the obligatory Thanksgiving pumpkin pie that barely gets touched except by your one great aunt who demands that you make it, fusses over it noisily, and then eats only a sliver. The smooth, sweet filling of this pie, made from the flesh of a freshly baked sugar pumpkin (a small and round pumpkin, with sweet, dark orange flesh) blended with rich evaporated milk, is balanced to perfection by the aromatic crust that is crisp but not brittle. Dig in.

CRUST

½ cup all-purpose gluten-free flour

¼ teaspoon xanthan gum

⅓ cup granulated sugar

2 cups finely ground **Ginger Cookies** (page 206)

1 stick (8 tablespoons) unsalted butter, melted and cooled

¼ cup mashed pumpkin purée (from baked sugar pumpkin in filling, below)

FILLING

1 sugar pumpkin (cut, seeded, and baked for 40 minutes at 350°F, the flesh pureed until smooth)

2 extra-large eggs

1 cup packed brown sugar

1 tablespoon all-purpose gluten-free flour

½ teaspoon kosher salt

2½ teaspoons pumpkin pie spice

1 (12–ounce) can evaporated milk (low-fat is fine, nonfat is not)

1. To make the crust, grease well a 9-inch pie plate with unsalted butter and set it aside.

2. In a medium-size bowl, stir together the flour, xanthan gum, granulated sugar, cookie crumbs, butter, and pumpkin purée, and blend well. Press the mixture into the bottom and sides of the pie plate. Cover with plastic wrap and chill

for at least 1 hour and up to overnight. Before the crust is ready to be baked, pre-heat the oven to 325°F. Once the crust has been chilled, remove the plastic wrap from the pie shell, cover the crust with foil to prevent burning, place it in the preheated oven, and bake for 10 minutes, no more. Cool completely.

3. To make the filling, preheat the oven to 450°F. In a large bowl, combine the remaining pumpkin puree, the eggs, brown sugar, flour, salt, pumpkin pie spice, and evaporated milk, blending well after each addition. Pour the filling into the cooled, baked shell. Place the pie in the preheated oven and bake for 10 minutes, then turn down the oven temperature to 350°F, and bake for another 45 to 60 minutes, or until a toothpick inserted into the center of the pie comes out clean.

4. Cool the pie to room temperature and refrigerate overnight. Serve chilled.

Banana Cream Pie
with Graham Cracker Crust

MAKES 8 SERVINGS

This banana cream pie is easy as 1-2-3, but it does take at least that many steps. It's a special pie for a special occasion, because it requires deliberate advance planning. Even the graham cracker crust is extraordinary: the addition of a mashed banana makes the crust slightly moist and chewy. If you spring for the (admittedly expensive) whole vanilla bean to use in the custard, you shall be richly rewarded.

CRUST

2 cups finely ground **Graham Crackers** (page 214)

⅓ cup sugar

¼ cup mashed, ripe banana (about 1 banana)

6 tablespoons unsalted butter, melted and cooled

FILLING

½ cup sugar

⅓ cup cornstarch

¼ teaspoon kosher salt

½ cup heavy cream

2½ cups milk (low-fat is fine, nonfat is not)

3 extra-large egg yolks

1½ teaspoons pure vanilla extract (or 1 whole vanilla bean, split open with a sharp knife)

FOR LAYERING

4 ripe (but not overripe) bananas, sliced in ¼-inch disks

1. To make the crust, preheat your oven to 350°F. Grease well a 10-inch glass pie plate with unsalted butter and set it aside.

2. In a medium-size bowl, stir together the graham cracker crumbs, sugar, mashed banana, and butter and mix well. Press the cracker mixture into the bottom and sides of the pie plate. Cover with plastic wrap and chill for at least 30 minutes and up to overnight. Once chilled, remove the plastic wrap from the pie shell, place it in the preheated oven, and bake for 10 to 12 minutes, or until pale golden. Cool the crust completely.

3. To make the pie filling, in a medium saucepan, whisk together the sugar, cornstarch, and salt and gradually add the cream and milk in a steady stream, then the egg yolks one at a time, whisking constantly. If you're using a whole vanilla bean, add it to the saucepan, place the saucepan on the stove top, and turn on the heat to medium, still whisking constantly, until the mixture begins to simmer and thicken, which takes 7 to 8 minutes.

4. Once the custard has begun to form, remove the saucepan from the heat and add the vanilla extract (if not using a whole vanilla bean), whisking to combine. If you used a whole vanilla bean, with a sharp knife, scrape the seeds from the pod into the custard and stir to combine. Pour the custard into a large, flat bowl, place plastic wrap directly on the surface of the custard, and allow it to sit at room temperature until it has cooled, about 1 hour.

5. Once the custard has cooled completely, remove the plastic wrap and stir if necessary to smooth the consistency. Pour 1 cup of the custard on top of the graham cracker crust and spread to coat the crust evenly. Cover the custard with a single layer of sliced bananas and alternate custard and bananas once more.

6. Chill the pie in the refrigerator for at least 8 hours, until set. Serve chilled.

Brownie Pie

MAKES 6 SERVINGS

This rich chocolate pie makes a really lovely presentation. With its crackled top and deep chocolate color, it's a welcome finish to a meal. It makes a nice dessert to bring to someone's house, especially since it's rich enough that a small slice is all you really need.

6 tablespoons unsalted butter

3 cups semisweet chocolate chips

½ cup all-purpose gluten-free flour

¼ teaspoon xanthan gum

½ cup unsweetened Dutch-processed cocoa powder

⅓ teaspoon baking powder

¼ teaspoon kosher salt

3 extra-large eggs

1 cup sugar

½ teaspoon pure vanilla extract

½ cup sour cream (low-fat is fine, nonfat is not)

1. Preheat the oven to 350°F. Grease well a 9-inch pie plate (or tart pan with removable sides) with unsalted butter and set it aside.

2. Place the butter and the 2 cups of chocolate chips in a large bowl. Microwave at 30 second intervals, stirring well in between, until the chocolate is melted and the mixture is smooth. Set the chocolate mixture aside to cool.

3. While the chocolate is cooling, in a medium bowl, combine the flour, xanthan gum, cocoa powder, baking powder, and salt and set aside the dry ingredients.

4. To the large bowl with the chocolate mixture, add the eggs, sugar, and vanilla, beating well after each ingredient. Add the dry ingredients to the large bowl of batter and beat until well blended, reserving a few tablespoons of dry ingredients in a small bowl. Add the sour cream to the batter and beat until the

batter becomes thicker and a bit more elastic, which means you have activated the xanthan gum.

5. Toss the remaining 1 cup of chocolate chips with the reserved dry ingredients, and add the chocolate chips to the batter. Stir the batter to evenly distribute the chocolate chips throughout.

6. Pour the batter into the prepared pie plate and, with wet fingers, smooth the top. Cover with foil and place the pie in the center of the preheated oven and bake for 35 to 40 minutes. Uncover and bake for another 5 minutes, or until a toothpick inserted into the center of the pie comes out mostly clean. Remove the pie from the oven and cool completely before serving. Slice into wedges and serve.

Classic Apple Pie

MAKES 1 PIE

It seems that people who shy away from pie making are put off mostly by the thought of making the crust. But hopefully now you've mastered the **Sweet Pastry Crust** (page 39) and are a true believer. After that, this pie is smooth sailing. Peeling, coring, and slicing the apples can be a bit time-consuming, but the more you do it, the easier and quicker it gets. We go to a beautiful orchard every fall for apple picking and then come home and make fresh apple pies. I always freeze, unbaked, at least one assembled pie to use come Thanksgiving, and the rest are gone in an instant. The house smells like a dream.

1 recipe **Sweet Pastry Crust** (page 39)

5 McIntosh or Granny Smith apples, peeled, cored, and sliced

½ cup sugar

1 tablespoon cornstarch

½ teaspoon pure vanilla extract

½ teaspoon ground cinnamon

¼ teaspoon kosher salt

1. Grease a 9-inch pie plate with unsalted butter and set it aside.

2. Separate the pastry crust into two disks. Roll each disk between two pieces of plastic wrap until it is about ⅛ inch thick. Carefully remove one of the sheets of plastic wrap from one of the sheets of dough and line the prepared pie plate with the dough, exposed side down. Gently press the dough into the pie plate, with as much overhang as there is naturally, and place the pie plate, covered in the remaining sheet of plastic wrap, into the refrigerator. Place the other flat sheet of dough in the refrigerator, too. Allow the dough to chill while you make the filling (or for at least 20 minutes).

3. Preheat the oven to 375°F. In a large bowl, place the apples, sugar, cornstarch, vanilla, cinnamon, and salt and stir to coat the apples.

4. Once chilled, remove the pie plate from the refrigerator, gently pull off the top layer of plastic wrap, and pour the apple mixture into the pie shell, piling

the apples a bit higher in the center of the pie. Remove the remaining dough from the refrigerator and carefully remove one of the sheets of plastic wrap. With the final sheet of plastic wrap still attached, moving slowly and purposefully (offering a little prayer right here if you are so inclined never hurt anyone), drape the second sheet of dough over the top of the pie, and remove the final piece of plastic wrap. Cinch the top and bottom pie shells together, pinching gently all around the pie plate.

5. With a very sharp knife, make two ½-inch cuts near the center of the top pie shell to allow steam to escape. Cover the entire pie, both top and bottom, with foil. We want the pie filling to steam the apples super soft before we peel back the foil and brown the crust. (At this point, the unbaked pie can be frozen and baked at another time.)

6. Place the pie on a rimmed baking sheet and in the middle of the preheated oven, and bake, covered, for 1 hour. Uncover the top of the pie and bake for another 10 to 15 minutes, until the crust is nicely browned. Allow to cool about 30 minutes, or more, before serving.

Apple Crisp

MAKES 6 TO 8 SERVINGS

Making this apple crisp is almost as easy as making applesauce, which itself is a great use of apples that have begun to show signs of age. Once they're peeled, cored, sliced, and cooked down either in a pot on the stove top or in the oven tucked under an apple crisp, no one minds if the apples were a little bruised or browned. I won't tell.

FILLING

5 to 6 apples, peeled, cored and sliced thinly (Empire and Granny Smith work well)

1 teaspoon ground cinnamon

2 tablespoons sugar

TOPPING

1 stick plus 2 tablespoons (10 tablespoons) unsalted butter, at room temperature

1 cup sugar

1 extra-large egg, slightly beaten

2 teaspoons pure vanilla extract

1½ cups all-purpose gluten-free flour

½ teaspoon xanthan gum

¼ cup gluten-free oats (can be replaced by an additional ¼ cup all-purpose gluten-free flour
   plus ⅛ teaspoon xanthan gum)

1 cup chopped walnuts or pecans (optional)

1. Preheat your oven to 350°F. Grease a 9-inch pie plate with unsalted butter and set it aside.

2. To make the filling, combine the apples, cinnamon, and sugar, and stir to combine well. You can toss the apples with the cinnamon and sugar right in the pie plate. Place the filling in the prepared pie plate, piled toward middle of the plate.

3. To make the topping, in a large bowl, blend the butter and sugar until light and fluffy. Add the egg and vanilla and blend well. Add the flour, xanthan gum,

and oats and beat the batter well until it becomes thicker and a bit more elastic. Add the walnuts, if using, and stir to distribute them evenly through the dough. The mixture should be very thick. Cover the apples with topping, spreading it evenly with wet hands.

4. Cover the pie plate with foil, place it in the center of the preheated oven, and bake for 35 minutes. Remove the foil and bake for another 15 to 20 minutes, until the topping is lightly golden brown. Cool at least 20 minutes before serving.

Cheesecake with Butter Cookie Crust

MAKES 6 TO 8 SERVINGS

I adore good cheesecake, which this most certainly is. This recipe makes a beautiful, golden crust, and the rich filling is made extra special with mascarpone cheese and fresh lemon juice and zest. The crust must be blind baked and allowed to cool completely before filling it, steps I encourage you to do a day or so ahead of time, just to make things entirely more pleasant.

CRUST

1 stick (8 tablespoons) unsalted butter, at room temperature

¼ cup sugar

½ cup all-purpose gluten-free flour

¼ teaspoon xanthan gum

½ cup finely ground **Butter Cookies** (page 202)

FILLING

1½ pounds (24 ounces) cream cheese (low-fat is fine, nonfat is not), at room temperature

1 cup mascarpone cheese

1½ cups sugar

3 extra-large eggs

Juice and finely grated zest of 1 lemon

1. Preheat the oven to 350°F. Grease a 9-inch pie plate with unsalted butter and set it aside.

2. To make the crust, cream together the butter and the sugar until light and fluffy. Add the flour, xanthan gum, and ground Butter Cookies. Mix until all the ingredients are completely blended together.

3. Press the mixture into the bottom of the prepared pie plate. Bake in the preheated oven for about 20 minutes (until golden). Cool completely. In the meantime, make the filling.

4. In a large bowl, beat the cream cheese alone until whipped-looking. Add the mascarpone cheese and the sugar, then the eggs one at a time until well blended. Add in the lemon juice and zest and beat to combine.

5. Pour the filling into the cooled crust and smooth the top. Fill a large oven-proof dish (I use a 9 x 12-inch Pyrex dish) with water about halfway and place it on the bottom rack of the preheated oven. Place the cheesecake on the middle rack. Bake for about 1 hour, until the cake is set. If you shimmy the plate a bit, the cheesecake shouldn't seem loose.

6. Remove the cheesecake from the oven, allow it to cool to room temperature, and then refrigerate it overnight (or for at least 5 to 6 hours). Serve chilled.

Chocolate Chip Brownies

MAKES 16 BROWNIES

We couldn't very well have a cookbook of basics without having a recipe for brownies. These are your classic brownies, dense, rich, and chewy as the day is long.

1 stick (8 tablespoons) unsalted butter, at room temperature

12 ounces semi-sweet chocolate chips, separated into 8-ounce and 4-ounce portions

1¼ cups sugar

3 extra-large eggs

1 cup all-purpose gluten-free flour

½ teaspoon xanthan gum

¼ cup Dutch-processed unsweetened cocoa powder

½ teaspoon baking powder

½ teaspoon kosher salt

1. Preheat the oven to 350°F. Line an 8-inch square baking pan with two criss-crossed strips of parchment paper long enough to overhang all the sides of the pan. Butter the parchment paper as best you can. As long as the parchment paper covers the entire inside surface of the pan, the brownies will come out of the pan well. Set the pan aside.

2. In a medium-size, microwave-safe bowl, combine the butter and 8 ounces of chocolate chips. Microwave for 1½ to 2 minutes, 30 seconds at a time, stirring well at each 30-second interval, until the chocolate is melted and smooth. Allow the chocolate mixture to cool slightly, for about 2 minutes.

3. Once the chocolate mixture has cooled, add to it the sugar and the eggs, one at a time, stirring to combine well after each addition. Next, add the flour, xanthan gum, cocoa powder, baking powder, and salt, reserving a few table-spoons of flour. Beat the batter well until it becomes thicker and a bit more elastic. Toss the remaining 4 ounces of chocolate chips with the reserved flour to coat the chocolate chips. Add the chocolate chips and remaining flour to the

batter, stirring until the chips are evenly distributed throughout the batter. Pour the batter into the prepared pan and smooth the top with a spatula or wet hands.

4. Place the pan in the preheated oven and bake for 25 to 30 minutes, until a toothpick inserted into the center comes out mostly clean, with a few moist crumbs attached. Cool the brownies in the pan for at least 30 minutes. Lift the brownies out of the pan with the overhung parchment paper, invert onto a cutting board, peel off the parchment paper, and slice into squares with a moistened serrated knife.

Shoestring Savings

Chocolate Chip Brownies

On a shoestring: $4.75 for 16 brownies

If you bought it: $16.00 for 16 brownies

Chocolate Chip Biscotti

MAKES 20 TO 24 COOKIES

Biscotti is the sort of crispy, crunchy cookie that just seems so quintessentially gluten-containing to me. So I think it's important to serve a nice batch of these twice-baked, no-butter cookies to any friends or family members who are still skeptical that foods can be both gluten-free and delightfully tasty. Nothing is entirely out of reach. Who needs gluten?

2 extra-large eggs, beaten

⅓ cup sugar

1 teaspoon pure vanilla extract

1¼ cups all-purpose gluten-free flour

½ teaspoon xanthan gum

1 teaspoon baking powder

¼ teaspoon kosher salt

½ cup semi-sweet chocolate chips

1. Preheat your oven to 350°F. Line rimmed baking sheets with parchment paper and set them aside.

2. In a large bowl, place the eggs, sugar, and vanilla and beat until well combined. Add the flour, xanthan gum, baking powder, and salt to the egg mixture, reserving a tablespoon of flour in a separate small bowl, and beat the ingredients well. Add the chocolate chips to the reserved flour, toss them to coat with flour, and then fold them into the batter until they are evenly distributed throughout.

3. Turn mixture onto a lightly floured surface and pat the dough into a loaf about 1 inch thick, 2½ inches wide, and about 7 inches long. Transfer the dough to a prepared baking sheet and place it in the center of the preheated oven. Bake for 20 to 25 minutes, until the loaf is firm to the touch and has risen a bit. Remove the baking sheet from the oven and allow it to cool completely. Reduce oven temperature to 300°F.

4. Once the biscotti loaf has cooled, with a large serrated knife, cut it on the diagonal into slices that are about ¼ inch thick. Arrange the slices in one layer on prepared baking sheets, about 1 inch apart. Place the baking sheets in the oven and bake again for 20 to 25 minutes until crisp and golden, turning over once during baking. Cool completely and enjoy.

Shoestring Savings

Chocolate Chip Biscotti

On a shoestring: $2.30 for about 22 cookies

If you bought it: $9.52 for 22 cookies

Vanilla Pudding

MAKES 4 TO 6 SERVINGS

Making pudding from scratch is no more difficult than making it from a prepared mix and requires almost no planning. Think of it like this: vanilla pudding is essentially just sitting there in your basic, well-stocked pantry, waiting for you to bring it to life. This recipe can easily make chocolate pudding by adding 2 ounces of semi-sweet chocolate to the pudding in step 3 below.

2½ cups milk (low-fat is fine, nonfat is not)
3 tablespoons cornstarch
⅔ cup sugar
⅛ teaspoon salt
2 tablespoons unsalted butter
1 teaspoon pure vanilla extract

1. Whisk together ½ cup of the milk and the cornstarch in a medium bowl until well blended (no lumps!). Set the bowl aside.

2. Bring the rest of the milk, sugar, and salt to a simmer in a medium-size pan over medium heat. Add the cornstarch mixture to the steaming pot. Cook, whisking often, until the mixture boils (4 or 5 minutes or so). Reduce the heat to a low simmer and whisk often, cooking for another 7 minutes until thickened.

3. Remove from heat and stir in the butter and vanilla until combined.

4. Pour the pudding into either five small dishes or one larger one, whichever you like. Cool in the refrigerator for at least a few hours, until firm. If you don't care for pudding skin, place plastic wrap right on top of the pudding before refrigerating and your pudding will be skinless.

Rice Pudding

MAKES 6 SERVINGS

Before I had tried good, creamy rice pudding, it sounded like madness to me. How could rice be dessert? When it's rice pudding, that's how. It's very similar to traditional **Vanilla Pudding** (page 232), but rice stands in for the cornstarch to make a creamy but substantial pudding.

2 cups water

⅛ teaspoon kosher salt

1 tablespoon unsalted butter

1 cup short-grain rice (like Arborio rice)

4 cups milk (low-fat is fine, nonfat is not)

½ cup sugar

2 teaspoons pure vanilla extract

⅛ teaspoon ground cinnamon

Shoestring Savings

Rice Pudding

On a shoestring: $2.40 for 6 servings

If you bought it: $3.50 for 6 servings

1. In a large saucepan, bring the water to a boil. Once the water is boiling, add the salt, butter, and rice, stirring to combine. Reduce the heat to a simmer and cook for about 10 to 15 minutes, or until the rice has absorbed most of the water, leaving behind no more than a bit of thick, starchy water. Be careful not to overcook the rice.

2. While the rice is cooking, in a separate, medium-size saucepan, combine the milk, sugar, vanilla, and cinnamon and cook over medium heat until the mixture is simmering. Once the rice in the separate saucepan is cooked, add the simmering milk mixture to the larger saucepan. Cook the rice and milk mixture over medium-low heat, stirring occasionally, until the rice has absorbed most of the milk mixture and the entire mixture has thickened and begins to appear pudding-like, 15 to 20 minutes more. The pudding will thicken as it cools and will set in the refrigerator.

3. Cool the pudding in the pan for about 15 minutes, then transfer to a large bowl and allow it to cool completely. Refrigerate until set, at least an hour.

Vanilla Hot Chocolate

MAKES 4 GENEROUS SERVINGS

The only easier way to make vanilla hot chocolate would be to open up a packet of the powdered stuff and add boiling water. But you're still boiling water if you do that, so why not make the good stuff? I like a mixture of cocoa powder and melted chocolate, and using a vanilla bean instead of vanilla extract (although more expensive) really makes this an occasional, and memorable, treat. The dash of table salt offsets the sweetness of the chocolate and really enhances the chocolate flavors.

5 tablespoons unsweetened Dutch-processed cocoa powder

6 cups milk (low-fat is fine, nonfat is not)

½ vanilla bean

⅛ teaspoon table (fine) salt

8 ounces semi-sweet chocolate chips

1. In a medium saucepan, whisk the cocoa powder into the milk until it is dissolved completely. Add the half vanilla bean to the milk mixture. Place the pan on the stove top and bring to a simmer over medium heat. Simmer gently for about 3 minutes, then remove the vanilla bean from the pan and set it aside. Add the salt and the chocolate to the milk mixture and stir until the chocolate melts completely. Turn the heat up to bring the mixture to a boil, whisking often.

2. With a sharp knife, split the vanilla bean on a flat surface without slicing all the way through. With the dull edge of the knife, scrape the seeds from inside the vanilla bean into the hot chocolate, whisking to combine.

3. Serve hot in mugs. Can be reheated.

Basic Chocolate Truffles

MAKES 30 TRUFFLES

Truffles are creamy and rich and make a very chic presentation. It's almost shameful how simple they are.

1 recipe **Chocolate Ganache** (page 236)
Unsweetened Dutch-processed cocoa powder or confectioner's sugar (for coating)

1. After making the recipe for Chocolate Ganache, cover the mixture and refrigerate until firm, about 2 hours or overnight.

2. Once the ganache has chilled, form into balls with a melon baller. Roll the balls in a coating of unsweetened cocoa powder or confectioner's sugar. Place the truffles on lined baking sheets, cover, and refrigerate until firm.

TOPPINGS

Chocolate Ganache

MAKES ABOUT ¾ CUP

Making ganache is like taking chocolate and turning it into a double agent. Although chocolate is solid at room temperature, and cream is liquid, when combined they meet each other in the middle. Chill ganache and you're halfway to truffles (see **Basic Chocolate Truffles**, page 235); pour it over a cake or cupcakes and it's a beautiful glaze.

6 ounces semi-sweet chocolate chips (or chopped chocolate)
¾ cup heavy cream
⅛ teaspoon kosher salt

1. Place the chocolate in a medium-size heatproof bowl and set it aside.
2. In a medium saucepan, bring the heavy cream to a gentle boil. Add the salt and stir to combine.
3. Pour the warm cream over the chocolate in a slow and steady stream, whisking constantly until the mixture is smooth. Allow the mixture to cool for about 2 minutes to use as a glaze.

Crumble Topping

MAKES ENOUGH CRUMBLE TOPPING FOR A 9-INCH CAKE

You'd be surprised how often you can use a good crumble topping. You can even bake it all by itself on a sheet pan in a single layer (at 350°F for 7 to 10 minutes), then sprinkle it over ice cream. The trick is to make sure that it's good and chilled before you bake it, so the crumbs don't melt and spread.

1 stick (8 tablespoons) unsalted butter, at room temperature
⅓ cup packed brown sugar
¼ cup granulated sugar
1 cup all-purpose gluten-free flour
½ teaspoon xanthan gum
⅛ teaspoon kosher salt

1. In a medium-size bowl, beat the butter and sugars until creamy. Add the flour, xanthan gum, and salt to the butter mixture and mix with a fork until coarse crumbs form.

2. Refrigerate the crumble mixture until firm, about 1 hour. Sprinkle evenly over whatever you are baking and bake according to recipe directions.

Basic White Frosting

MAKES ENOUGH FROSTING FOR AN 8-INCH, TWO-LAYER CAKE
OR 24 TO 36 STANDARD-SIZE CUPCAKES

The salt balances the sweetness of this frosting, which allows you to use enough confectioner's sugar to make proper frosting. It has a respectable consistency without being cloyingly sweet.

1 cup shortening (or 1 cup unsalted butter, softened, if the frosting needn't be white)
1 teaspoon pure vanilla extract (colorless, if the frosting must be white)
¼–½ teaspoon table (fine) salt
3–4 cups confectioner's sugar
2–4 tablespoons milk (anything but nonfat, and any nondairy milk will do)

1. In a large bowl (or in the bowl of an electric mixer fitted with the paddle attachment), beat the shortening (or butter) by hand until light and fluffy. Add the vanilla and ¼ teaspoon of the salt and beat to combine.

2. Add the confectioner's sugar, one cup at a time, beating well after each addition. Add the final cup more slowly, beating constantly, until you reach the desired consistency. Add the milk and beat well to smooth out the appearance of the frosting.

3. Taste a bit of frosting. Add the remaining ¼ teaspoon salt if you wish.

Citrus Glaze

MAKES ENOUGH GLAZE FOR 12 STANDARD-SIZE CUPCAKES

Lemon Cupcakes (page 184) have extra zip when iced with Citrus Glaze. The glaze is also delightful drizzled over **Pound Cake** (page 186).

1–1½ cups confectioner's sugar

2 tablespoons freshly squeezed citrus juice

1. Combine the confectioner's sugar and the lemon juice until smooth, adjusting the amount of confectioner's sugar to achieve the desired consistency. If you find that you have added too much sugar, just add a few drops of water to thin the glaze.

2. When using the glaze, place whatever cakes you are glazing on a wire rack, pour the glaze evenly over the top, and allow it to set. Chill glazed cakes in the refrigerator to set if your environment is humid.

Sour Cream Chocolate Frosting

MAKES ENOUGH FROSTING FOR AN 8-INCH, TWO-LAYER CAKE

Making my own dressings, frosting, and sauces is something I started doing many years ago. The ingredients that are essential to these staples not only have long shelf lives, but also are already part of an otherwise well-stocked pantry. And, of course, making them yourself means that you can modify the recipes to suit your personal tastes, and make only what you need. Good taste at a good price, with no waste.

1 cup semi-sweet chocolate chips
½ stick (4 tablespoons) unsalted butter
½ cup sour cream (low-fat is fine, nonfat is not)
1 teaspoon pure vanilla extract
¼ teaspoon table (fine) salt
1½–2 cups confectioner's sugar

1. Place the chocolate chips and butter in a large, microwave-safe bowl and microwave for 30 seconds at a time, stirring well after each 30-second cycle, until smooth and shiny.

2. Add the sour cream, vanilla, and salt to the chocolate mixture and mix by hand until smooth. Gradually add the confectioner's sugar, blending well, until spreadable.

Royal Icing

MAKES ABOUT 2½ CUPS, ENOUGH FOR 3 TO 4 DOZEN 2-INCH COOKIES

Royal icing begins to harden upon exposure to the air, so it should be used immediately or placed in an airtight container until you are ready to use it. Once you have used the icing as you have planned, whatever has been iced should be allowed to dry at room temperature completely, which may take several hours, before storing.

2 extra-large (pasteurized) egg whites (instead of pasteurized eggs, you can use Meringue Powder or an egg-replacer)
2 teaspoons freshly squeezed lemon juice
3 cups confectioner's sugar
Gel food coloring, if desired

1. In a large bowl, beat the egg whites with the lemon juice until well blended. Add the sugar and beat until smooth. The icing should be runny, but not thin like a liquid.

2. Add gel food coloring sparingly, blending well after each addition, until the desired color is reached.

Rolling Fondant

MAKES ENOUGH FONDANT FOR A 9-INCH ROUND, TWO-LAYER CAKE

Have you ever tried to make your child a birthday cake in the image of a beloved character? Too many times, I searched far and wide and finally found a cake mold in the shape of the character. Following the instructions on the mold, I baked the cake and decorated it with carefully dyed and piped frosting. I put a candle in and placed the cake on the table in front of the expectant birthday boy. He had no idea what it was. It was like some sort of impressionist painting: if you're sitting too close, you can't quite make it out properly. I was using the wrong medium.

Fondant, which just means "melting" in French, will give birth to the latent cake-decorating professional you know yourself to be. This recipe doesn't call for glycerine (which helps to keep the fondant from cracking, but can be a bit hard to find) or gelatin (which can be difficult to work with), all in the name of simplicity. Unused fondant can be stored in an airtight container for about 2 weeks, at room temperature (as long as you use shortening instead of butter) or in the refrigerator. Keep in mind that you will need some frosting, though, to spread on the cake first to help the fondant stay put once you place it on the cake.

Gluten-free nonstick cooking spray
½ cup (8 tablespoons) shortening (or an equal amount unsalted butter, at room temperature)
½ cup light corn syrup
¼ teaspoon pure vanilla extract (colorless)
¼ teaspoon table (fine) salt
1 pound (about 3¼ cups) confectioner's sugar
Gel food coloring, if desired

1. Coat the bowl of your stand mixer with nonstick cooking spray to prevent the ingredients from sticking. On medium speed, using the paddle attachment, beat the shortening with the corn syrup, then add in the vanilla extract and the salt.

2. Coat the dough hook attachment with nonstick cooking spray and swap out the paddle for the dough hook. Turn the mixer on low speed and slowly add most of the confectioner's sugar until a stiff paste forms (about 3 or 4 minutes). If the dough is noticeably sticky, add in the rest of the confectioner's sugar until the dough is smooth. Mix in the (optional) gel food coloring until you reach the desired color. Wrap the fondant in plastic wrap and place it in the refrigerator for about 15 minutes, until firm.

3. Once the fondant has chilled, place it between two large pieces of plastic wrap very lightly dusted with confectioner's sugar and roll until it is between ⅛ and ¼ inch thick. After rolling, place it in the refrigerator once more to chill, if necessary, for proper firmness. You want the fondant to be relatively strong and stretchy. Before draping over a chilled cake, cover the cake with a very thin film of frosting, so the fondant stays in place.

4. To drape the fondant, remove and replace one sheet of the plastic wrap and remove and discard the other. Roll the side of the fondant covered in plastic wrap around the rolling pin and unroll it on top of the surface you are decorating. Once the fondant is in place, remove the final sheet of plastic wrap, and voilà.

Metric Conversions

The recipes in this book have not been tested with metric measurements, so some variations might occur.

Remember that the weight of dry ingredients varies according to the volume or density factor: 1 cup of flour weighs far less than 1 cup of sugar, and 1 tablespoon doesn't necessarily hold 3 teaspoons.

General Formula for Metric Conversion

Ounces to grams	ounces $\times$ 28.35 = grams
Grams to ounces	grams $\times$ 0.035 = ounces
Pounds to grams	pounds $\times$ 453.5 = grams
Pounds to kilograms	pounds $\times$ 0.45 = kilograms
Cups to liters	cups $\times$ 0.24 = liters
Fahrenheit to Celsius	(°F − 32) $\times$ 5 ÷ 9 = °C
Celsius to Fahrenheit	(°C $\times$ 9) ÷ 5 + 32 = °F

Volume (Liquid) Measurements

1 teaspoon = ⅙ fluid ounce = 5 milliliters
1 tablespoon = ½ fluid ounce = 15 milliliters
2 tablespoons = 1 fluid ounce = 30 milliliters
¼ cup = 2 fluid ounces = 60 milliliters
⅓ cup = 2⅔ fluid ounces = 79 milliliters
½ cup = 4 fluid ounces = 118 milliliters
1 cup or ½ pint = 8 fluid ounces = 250 milliliters
2 cups or 1 pint = 16 fluid ounces = 500 milliliters
4 cups or 1 quart = 32 fluid ounces = 1,000 milliliters
1 gallon = 4 liters

Volume (Dry) Measurements

¼ teaspoon = 1 milliliter

½ teaspoon = 2 milliliters

¾ teaspoon = 4 milliliters

1 teaspoon = 5 milliliters

1 tablespoon = 15 milliliters

¼ cup = 59 milliliters

⅓ cup = 79 milliliters

½ cup = 118 milliliters

⅔ cup = 158 milliliters

¾ cup = 177 milliliters

1 cup = 225 milliliters

4 cups or 1 quart = 1 liter

½ gallon = 2 liters

1 gallon = 4 liters

Weight (Mass) Measurements

1 ounce = 30 grams

2 ounces = 55 grams

3 ounces = 85 grams

4 ounces = ¼ pound = 125 grams

8 ounces = ½ pound = 240 grams

12 ounces = ¾ pound = 375 grams

16 ounces = 1 pound = 454 grams

Linear Measurements

½ in = 1½ cm

1 inch = 2½ cm

6 inches = 15 cm

8 inches = 20 cm

10 inches = 25 cm

12 inches = 30 cm

20 inches = 50 cm

Oven Temperature Equivalents, Fahrenheit (F) and Celsius (C)

100°F = 38°C

200°F = 95°C

250°F = 120°C

300°F = 150°C

350°F = 180°C

400°F = 205°C

450°F = 230° C

Acknowledgments

To my agent, Brandi Bowles, who saw my blog in that *New York Times* article, reached out, and together we hit the ground running. Every comment, every gentle critique, every piece of advice is always spot on.

To my editor, Katie McHugh, who *really* pores over every word of every chapter, and every recipe. She makes everything better, keeping my voice, but adjusting the pitch. Her dedication is so uncommon, she's even gluten-free herself.

To all the professionals at Perseus Books, who really know their stuff, which came in handy since I didn't know the ropes.

To my children, who ate a lot of food. And even timed their growth spurts to happen just in time for the more intense periods of recipe testing.

To my husband, who ate a lot, too, including the recipe fiascoes that the kids wouldn't eat, and insisted upon integrity at every stage of the process.

To Sue Goldstein, who is always looking out for my family, in all the best ways.

To my blog readers, whose kind words are often timed just perfectly, right around misadventures in the ol' test kitchen. And whose queries and challenges only made me better.

Index

Nick Saraco Photography

About the Author

Nicole Hunn is the personality behind the *Gluten-Free on a Shoe-string* blog, featured in the *New York Times* and MSN Money. She lives with her family in Westchester County, New York. Visit her website at http://glutenfreeonashoestring.com.